AN INTRODUCTION TO
GAME THEORY

MARTIN J. OSBORNE

AN INTRODUCTION TO
GAME THEORY

INTERNATIONAL EDITION

New York   Oxford
OXFORD UNIVERSITY PRESS
2009

Oxford University Press, Inc., publishes works that further Oxford University's
objective of excellence in research, scholarship, and education.

Oxford New York
Auckland Cape Town Dar es Salaam Hong Kong Karachi
Kuala Lumpur Madrid Melbourne Mexico City Nairobi
New Delhi Shanghai Taipei Toronto

With offices in
Argentina Austria Brazil Chile Czech Republic France Greece
Guatemala Hungary Italy Japan Poland Portugal Singapore
South Korea Switzerland Thailand Turkey Ukraine Vietnam

Published by Oxford University Press, Inc.
198 Madison Avenue, New York, New York 10016
http://www.oup.com

Oxford is a registered trademark of Oxford University Press

Library of Congress Cataloging-in-Publication Data

ISBN 978-0-19-532248-4 (paper)

REPORT OF THE COMMITTEE

ON THE

LESSONS OF THE GREAT WAR

APPOINTED ON 43/Training/1363

REPORTED ON 43/Training/1451

THE WAR OFFICE,
October, 1932

[A 3629]

The Naval & Military Press Ltd

Published by
The Naval & Military Press Ltd
5 Riverside, Brambleside, Bellbrook
Industrial Estate, Uckfield, East Sussex,
TN22 1QQ England

Tel: +44 (0) 1825 749494
Fax: +44 (0) 1825 765701
www.naval-military-press.com
www.military-genealogy.com

CONSTITUTION OF THE COMMITTEE.

President.

Lieut.-General W. M. St. G. KIRKE, C.B., C.M.G., D.S.O.

Members.

Major-General C. C. ARMITAGE, C.M.G., D.S.O.
Major-General A. W. BARTHOLOMEW, C.M.G., C.B.E., D.S.O.
Major-General B. D. FISHER, C.B., C.M.G., D.S.O.
Colonel (temp. Brigadier) R. G. H. HOWARD-VYSE, C.M.G.,
    D.S.O.
Major-General J. KENNEDY, C.B., C.M.G., D.S.O.
Colonel (temp. Brigadier) A. J. McCULLOCH, D.S.O., D.C.M.,
    A.D.C.
Major-General A. E. McNAMARA, C.B., C.M.G., D.S.O.

Secretary.

Major A. R. SELBY (S.D. 4).

TERMS OF REFERENCE.

The Committee will investigate and report upon the following questions : —

   (*a*) What are the principal lessons to be derived from our experiences in the several theatres of the Great War as disclosed by the official histories and reports?
   (*b*) Have these lessons been correctly and adequately applied in Field Service Regulations and other training manuals, and in our system of training generally?

WORKING DATA.

The Committee in their review should cover not only the principal strategical and tactical lessons, but also the more important administrative lessons, and those lessons falling under the headings of training, organization, higher command and staff duties.

The subject will be examined in the light of the most probable types of operation in which our military forces are likely to be employed, as set out in Army Training Memorandum, No. 4A, of 1932, but the Committee will keep within its purview all the possible liabilities and not confine itself to the " Major Expedition ".

4

CONTENTS.

REPORT

NOTE BY THE PRESIDENT.

In view of the very wide scope of the enquiry to be covered I judged it best to decentralize the work, allotting campaigns to various officers.

Beyond meeting to arrange the general lines on which the reports should be drawn up by members of the Committee* and issuing a list of points which might repay investigation, no effective collaboration by the Committee as a whole was attempted in the earlier stages of our investigation.

The classes of campaign covered are so different, the personal experiences of the members of the Committee so wide and varied, that it seemed to me to be far better to give officers complete freedom to express their opinion, with the object of getting every point of view, in the hope that from them might emerge some lessons common to all and consequently of universal application.

The degree of unanimity displayed, both as to what are the most important lessons of the war and their implications in our organization and training, is greater than I had either hoped or anticipated, as will appear in the following pages.

These latter are an attempt to bring some of the lessons into bolder relief and to indicate possible directions in which the gaps between the lessons of the war on the one hand, and the training manuals, organization and equipment of the troops on the other, may be reduced.

This general report, however, by no means covers all the points raised in the various reports of members of the Committee,* and is incomplete without them.

They also serve a useful purpose in showing the difference in the points of view which naturally follow the study of campaigns under those differing conditions, which constitute the main difficulty of our problem.

---

* The following reports are being submitted separately (not printed) :—

  (i) Report on the Western Front, by Major-General A. E. McNamara, C.B., C.M.G., D.S.O.

  (ii) Report on the Western Front, by Major-General J. Kennedy, C.B., C.M.G., D.S.O.

  (iii) Report on Gallipoli, by Lieut.-General W. M. St. G. Kirke, C.B., C.M.G., D.S.O.

  (iv) Report on Palestine by Colonel (temp. Brigadier) A. J. McCulloch, D.S.O., D.C.M., A.D.C.

  (v) Report on Mesopotamia, by Major-General B. D. Fisher, C.B., C.M.G., D.S.O. and Major-General C. C. Armitage, C.M.G., D.S.O.

That a Committee of this nature, convened for a few months, would be able to indicate a clear-cut answer to problems which have formed the subject of close study by every General Staff for fourteen years was doubtless not expected. Should we have succeeded in giving any slight forward impulse towards the solution of any of them we shall not have laboured in vain.

W. KIRKE,
Lieut.-General.

A.—PEACE PREPARATION

1. WIDE STUDY BY THE GENERAL STAFF NECESSARY IN PEACE-TIME.

Prior to the Great War attention was focussed on the German military problem to the practical exclusion of possibilities in all other theatres, and the Dardanelles and Mesopotamian campaigns suffered thereby. Since the disappearance of the German menace in 1918, our plans have probably been more catholic in scope, but if, as seems possible, the German danger again comes to the fore our outlook may again become too limited.

2. IMPORTANCE OF CONTINUITY IN THE DIRECTION OF WAR.

That the Government should have confidence in the Chief of the Imperial General Staff and the staff which he controls is of vital importance, and never more so than in the early stages of a war. To change the Chief of the Imperial General Staff on or just before mobilization or to allow his staff to go to the front as was done in 1914 is an error.

Many of our difficulties and mistakes can be traced to this source. Periodical changes between officers at the War Office and the various fronts during the war were valuable for both. The same principle should be applied to trainers of troops.

3. NECESSITY FOR CENTRAL CONTROL.

All military operations must, under the supreme direction of the Cabinet, be controlled by the War Office, which alone can assess their relative priority in the distribution of the resources available.

The Civil authority on the spot has a not unnatural belief in its ability to run its own local war, and does not always welcome higher control. The Mesopotamian campaign was an outstanding example of this evil.

The question is likely to arise in an acute form in the case of a campaign on or across the Indian frontier, if it should require considerable reinforcements in men or material from Home at at a time when we have serious commitments elsewhere.

4. PREPARATIONS FOR MOBILIZATION AND EXPANSION.

The standard of readiness required of an Expeditionary Force depends mainly on political factors which a Committee such as ours cannot assess. On the answer to the political problem depend military factors such as the actual time permissible for mobilization, collection and preparation of sea transport, preparation of overseas bases, or accommodation in the areas of concentration, or deployment and so forth. It is for the General Staff to balance these various factors, remembering that the strength of a chain is its weakest link.

But our study has led us to one broad conclusion, which is that the British Army has always been inadequate to finish any serious war quickly, and there appears to be nothing in the present situation to disprove the theory that a large expansion of the peace-time Army will be required in any future emergency.

The implications are far too wide to be dealt with exhaustively, but a few points are mentioned in our reports, *e.g.*, expansion of army schools, mobilization of the Territorial Army, formation of machine gun units if none exist in peace, expansion of armoured fighting vehicle units, and a scientific system of recruitment. One of the mistakes made in the War was to permit large numbers of potential officers to be killed as private soldiers in 1914-15. Rationing of the available man-power both as regards quality and quantity from the earliest stages as between Industry and the Services is as necessary as in the case of other raw material of which the supply is limited. It is for the War Office to ensure that the proportion allotted to the Army is no squandered by putting square pegs into round holes.

In this connection it might be worth while to investigate the question whether the Officers Training Corps' curriculum at schools is made sufficiently interesting and instructive from the point of view of producing future officers.

5. NECESSITY FOR A CONTINUOUS STUDY OF SCIENTIFIC DEVELOPMENTS AS AFFECTING WAR.

A conscript Army, which is recruited from every class and profession, has an advantage over a purely professional Army such as ours in keeping abreast of modern scientific developments. The German " listening sets ", which were unmasked by the French and not by us, the development of gas from commercial dye plants, and the secret development of super-heavy artillery were cases in point. There is always the danger that the next war may find us surprised again by some new scientific weapon.

Close co-operation with civilian experts is therefore very necessary in peace-time, but is not easy to arrange. How far the ground is covered by the Mechanical Warfare Board, the Ordnance Committee, the Royal Engineer Board and similar bodies, is unknown to us, but we are strongly impressed with the importance of the problem.

6. The value of scientific developments for a small army such as ours.

On the other side of the picture is the vital importance of making use of any advantage with which science may present us for policing the Empire.

The armament of second-class or even semi-regular enemies is constantly improving while they retain their pristine advantages of numbers, mobility and ease of maintenance.

All the campaigns which we have studied impress on us the practical dangers to which our small forces will be exposed, if in addition to losing the invaluable help of gas, we are deprived of arms such as tanks, offensive aircraft, and to a less extent heavy artillery, which constitute almost our sole remaining advantages. We also regard with misgiving the placing of such powerful weapons in the hands of any but the most reliable troops.

7. Importance of forming a National Government.

A serious war cannot, in modern conditions, be brought to a successful conclusion unless it has the support of the nation as a whole.

The formation of a National Government is the natural corollary, and this system has been happily adopted by us in times of national emergency. But in 1914 its importance was not realized, with the result that the government was changed at a time which had unfortunate effects on at least one campaign (Gallipoli) owing to a hiatus in control at a critical moment.

The formation of a national and non-party government coincident with mobilization appears to be an essential measure.

If there is a possibility of air attack on London the question should be investigated of moving the seat of government North on the decision to mobilize.

B.—STRATEGY AND TACTICS

8. Importance of Administration.

The interdependence of policy and strategy is a truism which was not always realized in practice. The subject is beyond the scope of this Committee, but the next stage, *viz.*, the dependence of policy and strategy on administrative possibilities, proved a frequent stumbling block.

The civilian, working from a small map on which none of the real problems appeared, was apt to think that the soldier was raising unnecessary administrative difficulties to avoid operations in which he did not wish to engage. On occasions he had some justification for this belief. Sometimes the soldier was himself to blame, for not realizing or inadequately representing the full extent of what the real difficulties were—this appears to have been the case in Mesopotamia.

As in the Great War, the importance of supply in the class of operations in undeveloped countries, which the British Army may be called upon to carry out, cannot be over emphasized. To the soldier this is a platitude.

9. The Importance of Surprise.

As a result of our study we are impressed with the paramount importance of surprise both in attack and defence.

The disastrous results of failure to achieve surprise strategically were shown at Gallipoli and elsewhere, but this major aspect of the question is above the sphere of the ordinary officer, and altogether outside peace training.

Surprise in the attack.—Dealing first with tactical surprise in the attack we agree with the opinions expressed by Major-Generals Fisher and Armitage in their report on the Mesopotamian campaign, viz.:—

"The greatest lesson to be gathered from the world war is that no attack in modern war is feasible or likely to succeed against an enemy in position unless his resisting power has already been paralyzed either by:—

(*a*) Some form of surprise; or
(*b*) Preponderating fire, powerful enough to produce the effect of surprise."

Even the analysis above may be held to understate the value of surprise, because if the defence is not completely immobile the preponderance of the attackers' fire, however great, may, without surprise, be rendered valueless by a short withdrawal, as carried out at Rheims by the French in 1918. The anxiety lest the enemy should have adopted this stratagem will be recalled by all who had anything to do with our own great attacks.

It is unnecessary to labour the principle further, the practical questions being, firstly, how to train leaders in peace-time to plan in terms of surprise; secondly, how to train troops to carry out the preliminary moves essential to the plan; and thirdly, how to equip them so that they can strike quickly enough to gain full advantage from the initial surprise when gained.

Taking the first of these questions, it must be admitted that in peace-time operations the known location of formations prior to the opening of hostilities, the limitations of ground, water points and so on, do seriously reduce the possibility of surprise, in some stations even more than in others. Doubtless, as shown this training season, a good deal can be done to mitigate these handicaps if attention is concentrated on the subject. Added to them, however, is one factor which, more than any other, may well make it seem to a commander to be hardly worth while even trying to achieve surprise; viz., air observation carried out in conditions which amount to a command of the air never achieved by both and seldom by even one combatant in war. A palliative is suggested in para. 27.

Coming to the second question, viz., movement to ensure surprise, the increasing use of darkness to cover preliminary movements was a noteworthy feature of all campaigns, whether in trench or open warfare. These were carried out on a large scale and over considerable distances in our Eastern campaigns, favoured no doubt by conditions of comparatively good visibility. These same conditions also favoured the attacks by night on difficult objectives, which were a marked characteristic of the later operations in Palestine and Syria.

But the fact that night operations were eventually common to all theatres shows their great importance. And this is natural since without doubt the automatic small-arm weapon forms the great strength of the modern defensive, and anything which tends to blind it must be to the advantage of the attacker if he is suitably trained.

The conclusion is that movements by night may often be the only way of obtaining a tactical surprise, and attack by night the most economical way of crowning it by tactical victory.

It has been pointed out that many of the attacks on the Western Front owed their success to fog and this for the same reason, viz., the blinding of the defender's machine gunners. The first battle of Gaza was probably lost because we did not take advantage of a similar opportunity.

Since we cannot command fog nor always wait for darkness before moving, smoke has a special value as an adjunct to local tactical surprise. It impinges, however, on the third question, viz., how to exploit surprise. This means actual fighting, and can more suitably be considered under the "Attack" (para. 10).

We agree that the great importance of a cloak of obscurity, darkness, fog or artificial smoke should be stressed, and in our training more attention be paid to:—

      (a) Moving at night on wide frontages;
      (b) Working in foggy weather;
      (c) The use of the compass.

In conclusion we are of opinion that our training manuals require to emphasize more strongly the vital importance of surprise and of the indirect approach and we are in agreement with Brigadier McCulloch's suggestion to add to F.S.R., II, Sec. 25 (2), a sentence to the following effect:—

"A Commander who selects the offensive and fails to surprise his opponent has lost the main advantage which the offensive confers."

Surprise in the defence.—Its importance is categorically stated in F.S.R., II, Sec. 78 (3), but the absolute priority given to securing ground observation for the artillery often has the effect of forcing the small-arm defence into exposed positions, and making the whole dispositions of the defence too obvious.

As the hidden machine gun is the greatest asset possessed by the defence, whereas the artillery has an alternative means of observation from the air, it is for consideration whether sometimes we do not lose more than we gain by the selection of obvious defensive positions with consequent exposure of the machine gun dispositions. Although in the war surprise was persistently sought and often realized in the attack, curiously enough in defence we seldom made any attempt to secure it. Though, as previously mentioned, fear of enemy withdrawal on the eve of our attacks often caused us intense anxiety, the propriety of adopting the same tactics ourselves to neutralize his attacks was slow in being realized. It is true now that F.S.R., II, Sec. 80 (3) and (5), and I.T., II, Sec. 20 (4) and (5), do include in the duties of outpost or other advanced troops the positive rôle of deception in addition to the more negative rôles of gaining time and giving warning, but only in F.S.R., II, Sec. 88 (4), dealing with the protracted defence, is the former strongly emphasized.

Whatever the precept, however, the fact remains that our practice during the war did not, and our training during peace does not, usually pay sufficient attention to surprise in defence.

In consequence our methods are apt to be too stereotyped, which again tends to produce the same weakness in our methods of attack.

The Committee do not wish it to be thought that they advocate an indeterminate or fluid form of defence, over extended in depth, such as was practised just after the war. Let there be no uncertainty in the minds of the defence as to what has to be defended to the last round and man, but do not let our dispositions be so stereotyped and immobile as to be obvious to the enemy.

10. ATTACK.

In 1914 the scales were already weighted in favour of the defence, and as the war proceeded the progressive increase in automatic weapons accentuated its superiority in all theatres of war, in spite of every attempt to redress the balance.

Is, then, the great lesson of the war that we should always try to act on the defensive, whatever the fifth principle of war may say to the contrary?

Great though the advantages of the defensive may be, in practice we know that our small army must be able to strike quickly and effectively, and that this principle is particularly important in Eastern theatres.

If, then, the Committee have concentrated their attention mainly on the offensive it is not because they advocate it on all occasions, but because it is by far the most difficult operation of war in modern conditions, and because it is towards its solution that all measures of reorganization or re-equipment should primarily be directed. Reduced to its simplest terms the problem is how to knock out or neutralize the unlocated machine gun.

Conditions naturally vary according to terrain and class of enemy, and there is this measure of comfort that usually the equipment of the enemy varies directly with the development of communications, and consequently with supply and maintenance.

The experiences of the war proved that, given plenty of time and ammunition and a rigid and located defence, a " break in " with overwhelming artillery support was possible.

But, as in 1914, none of these conditions may obtain in mobile warfare in the early stages of a campaign, and at present, even in an advanced guard action, hostile machine guns tend to produce immediate paralysis.

Various solutions have been advanced in the reports on the several campaigns by members of the Committee, the chief of these being—

(a) An increase of artillery;
(b) An increase of armoured fighting vehicles;
(c) An increase in mobility of the infantry soldier;
(d) To provide infantry with its own means for producing covering fire by mortars.

Each of these suggestions is supported by experiences of the late war, and a selection of one or other depends *inter alia* on factors outside the cognisance of this Committee, chief of which are the limitations imposed by obligatory garrisons and the normal peace-time police duty of the British Army.

Some remarks on the suggestions above may not, however, be out of place.

Alternative (a). Increase of Artillery.

We are impressed by the difficulties of providing adequate covering fire by artillery sufficiently quickly to meet many of the problems of open warfare. The pause during the elaboration of a fire plan leaves the enemy free to manœuvre, and when the fire plan is ready it may no longer be applicable. Such methods may well put a tame finish to a promising situation created by manœuvre and surprise. This question of speeding up the organization of artillery fire plans has been closely studied, but so far the results have not been very encouraging.

Our only constructive suggestions are that—

(i) If the dominating weapon in an attack is the artillery, and time is of primary importance, the Commander should give full weight to the importance of choosing a line of advance for his attack which will give the greatest scope to the artillery in the time available. F.S.R. does not bring out this principle because it has not quite got away from the old adage that " the infantry is the arm which wins battles ". Many Commanders do not understand the technical difficulties in firing a moving barrage or series of concentrations, which entail " switches " as well as " lifts ".

(ii) Covering fire will often have to take the form of observed fire as stated in I.T., Vol. II, Sec. 9 (4), and, if time is to be saved, directed from observation posts already established by the advanced guard.

It follows that observation parties should be as numerous and as well forward as possible so as to take every advantage of possibilities for putting down observed fire.

(iii) Survey methods should be regarded as a most valuable adjunct in conditions where time is available, but not as a primary method to be introduced on every possible occasion, favourable or unfavourable.

Assuming that an increase of artillery is one answer to the problem, though not necessarily the best, how is the increase to be made? We may at once dismiss any idea of increasing the size of a division which is already too large. The suggestion to convert the Light Brigade into a normal part of the Divisional Artillery avoids this and effects an increase of 16 to 25 per cent. according to whether the 3·7-inch howitzers are retained or are replaced by a full Field Artillery Brigade. This step necessitates, however, as an essential corollary, the addition of infantry " artillery " in the shape of mortars which will be discussed later.

We recognize that the limiting factor here, as always, is finance, but investigations in this direction are outside our terms of reference.

Alternative (b). Increase of armoured fighting vehicles.

This alternative is attractive because covering fire can be produced without elaborate fire plans, and because it speeds up the whole tempo of the attack. Moreover, the fact that the tank combines the power both to blind and penetrate the defence—the rôles formerly allotted to artillery and to infantry and cavalry respectively—must in suitable country enormously simplify the organization of attack.

And it is just this simplification which appears to be so urgently necessary. The performances of the tank on the Western Front and even more what they could obviously have done in other theatres place their value beyond a shadow of doubt.

One objection put forward, that expansion should be postponed until war is imminent owing to constant improvement in design, does not appear to us to be an adequate reason for delay.

Alternative (c). Increase in mobility of the infantry soldier.

All the campaigns which we have studied lead us to the same conclusion, that the load carried by the infantry soldier must be reduced.

We also wish to see the equipment simplified, but like any other collection of officers we are not unanimous as to how this should be done.

We are, however, agreed that no measure of this kind will, by itself, restore the requisite superiority to the attack, even in difficult or broken ground.

Alternative (d). Providing infantry with its own means for producing covering fire by mortars.

The addition of mortars is another method of increasing the divisional artillery by relieving it of close support duties, and from that point of view is advantageous.

The majority of the Committee is in favour of this course, but it has the disadvantage that it is contrary to the principle of simplifying the equipment and ammunition supply of the infantry battalion, and this dilemma we may well leave to higher authority for adjustment. A possible solution, acceptable to all members of the Committee, is to incorporate a detachment of mortars in a divisional unit such as a machine gun battalion.

Our reading of history leads us to believe that it will be necessary to employ independent machine gun units in war, and that if the present organization is retained, a proportion of machine guns from infantry battalions might well go into them as a start.

The difficulties of carrying out such a measure in peace-time owing to obligatory garrisons have hitherto prevented the maintenance of machine gun battalions in peace-time. But the example of the two armoured car regiments shows that these difficulties have possibly been exaggerated.

We are definitely of opinion, however, that the possibility of converting certain battalions into heavy machine gun units in peace should take a leading place in any future scheme of reorganization, particularly if that scheme includes the re-armament of the normal infantry battalions with a lighter form of machine gun.

The advantages of such a measure from the point of view of the infantry battalion are that it would: —

    (i) Simplify the equipment of infantry battalions, making them more mobile and more suited to world-wide employment than at present.

   (ii) Simplify the organization of infantry battalions by re-introducing 4 homogeneous companies, each with its own light machine guns.

  (iii) Simplify the training of infantry by substituting one automatic for two—the Lewis and Vickers guns.

  (iv) Avoid the breaking up of infantry machine gun companies for such duties as barrages, reinforcement of other battalions, protection of headquarters, and similar employment necessitating separation from the parent unit for which the sub-units are not administratively organized.

The machine gun battalion, mechanized and suitably organized into sub-units, including anti-tank sub-units capable of independent action, could provide: —

    (i) A means of avoiding a change on mobilization, which is otherwise probable.

   (ii) A source from which demands for protection by headquarters could be met.

  (iii) An ideal accompaniment to armoured units for consolidating ground won and securing a base for a further bound.

  (iv) A simple organization for training machine-gunners in peace and war.

   (v) A powerful and highly mobile reserve of fire-power.

As a whole the measure would create a more suitable and flexible organization, and this in the face of our uncertain war problems seems to us to clinch the argument.

We are convinced that this is the solution to many of the present difficulties in connection with infantry organization.

We are definitely of the opinion that the machine gun battalions should remain in the infantry fold, and not be formed into a machine gun corps. Such small corps are an unnecessary encumbrance in times of changing organization. We already have too many of them.

As a separate question the necessity for providing infantry with effective protection against armoured fighting vehicles is of vital importance if the enemy is likely to be equipped with such weapons. In Europe he assuredly will be, and there is no certainty that a major expedition further East may not find itself exposed to tank attack.

11. How to convert a " break in " into a " break through."

We are convinced that this is the most important and difficult question with which the war presents us, and that it is the one which is least adequately dealt with in our training manuals or practised in our peace training. We use the term " break through " to indicate the carrying through of an attack to a complete decision. This applies equally to every form of attack, whether frontal, flank or counter-attack.

Its consideration logically divides itself into the following compartments : —

(i) Exercise of command, dependent on information and power to issue orders, which again requires;

(ii) Good communications;

(iii) Reserves at the disposal of the commander sufficiently powerful and mobile to take advantage of the opportunity created by the " break in," including transport to maintain them.

Each of these raises a number of subsidiary questions, and only a brief summary is here possible.

(a) Exercise of Command.

(i) The high standard of physical fitness required for active command in the field—not normally a characteristic of advancing years—was not always recognized.

(ii) Headquarters were frequently kept too far back.

(iii) There was a tendency to throw responsibility on to subordinates which should have been shouldered by the higher command, more adequately staffed to discharge it.

(b) *Communications.*

This appears to be the crux of the matter, because if a commander does not know what is happening he cannot make any useful plans. Even if he forms a plan he cannot put it into effect unless he can issue the necessary orders.

This state of affairs was normally accepted and led to plans being made for the continuance of operations in situations which did not eventuate. Once the battle was joined the higher command ceased to influence it.

The general air of uncertainty and absence of command was sometimes attributable to destruction of cable communications by artillery, and it is argued that the increase of track vehicles will be quite as destructive in open warfare.

What is the solution? One palliative obviously is to get headquarters further forward, or to give commanders the power of themselves going forward quickly and in reasonable safety. This means armoured command vehicles. In the same order of ideas is the proposal to make the higher commander responsible for maintaining communication with his subordinates. F.S.R., II, Sec. 139 (2) (i), so places responsibility whereas sub-paras. (iv) and (v) divide it.

We also advocate a more extended use of liaison personnel within the battalion, whose sole duties would be to report on the situation as it affects both the enemy and our own troops. The introduction of motor cycles in the battalion for the speeding up of intercommunication within the battalion is also desirable.

At the same time we recommend the development of wireless and the scrapping of cable altogether in front of brigade headquarters, except for artillery. In making this proposal we must sound a note of warning. During the later operations in Palestine W/T seems to have been effective, but at the first battle of Gaza the more powerful Turkish W/T installation is said to have jammed all the field stations on which the British depended. This might happen again unless the experts have devised a remedy.

A further suggestion is to make much more use of the Royal Air Force as a means of exercising command. Looking back on the many directions in which the ground troops were helped by the air during the war, it is for consideration whether the Army is deriving all the benefits which should accrue from modern development in aircraft. For instance, the trial of " light " aircraft for intercommunication purposes might prove a fruitful line of experiment.

Lastly comes the suggestion that the whole plan of battle might be simplified by greater reliance on armoured fighting vehicles, their direction and control being assisted by aircraft communications.

Unless a solution can be found to this question of inter-communication, there appear to be only two alternatives, the first being to delegate authority completely to subordinate commanders, trusting to their initiative in conformity with general instructions; the second being to revert to the highly stereotyped plans of the Western Front.

Of the two the former is far the better, and since in the case of the forward bodies it will often be unavoidable, our commanders should be trained accordingly.

But it is not a satisfactory substitute for the continuous control from above which constitutes the difference between generalship and a mere dog fight; between reinforcing success and hammering away at failure in the manner so adversely commented upon in the Official Histories of the War.

(c) Method and means required to complete a "break through".

The only successful example dealt with in the official histories so far published is the battle of Megiddo. Here the initial stages were effected by a surprise attack with infantry under comparatively over-whelming artillery support, developed by skilful and rapid manœuvre of infantry and artillery on normal pre-war lines to a limited distance, and completed by a powerful force of cavalry. Infantry followed as far as their legs would carry them to occupy the ground won and mop-up, whilst aircraft contributed to the dispersion of the already dis-organized and retreating enemy.

The results of our attempts to put the cavalry through on the Western Front are well known. Their arrival on the scene in large masses in accordance with a pre-arranged time-table usually hindered rather than helped the infantry because they were so easily stopped by machine guns and the ground was against them. At Cambrai the chances were better but the ground again was unfavourable. On 8th August, 1918, in conjunction with tanks they produced a certain effect.

In their partial " break through " of 1918 the Germans having practically no tanks* or cavalry relied on infantry supported by artillery and their own mortars. The infantry successfully made the necessary " hole " and then advanced to the limit of their marching powers, but they proved to be inadequate for complete success, owing to lack of the necessary mobility.

Before entirely writing off mounted troops for such operations it might be worth considering whether cavalry in large numbers could have got through with or even without tanks, and what would have been the result had they done so.

---

* It was not until the end of April, 1918, that German tanks first made their appearance at Villers Bretonneaux.

In any case it is clear that infantry reserves moving on their feet are too slow either in reaching the point where initial success has been gained, or in pushing forward sufficiently rapidly to forestall enemy reinforcements.

There is no difference of opinion but that the armoured fighting vehicles combine the necessary punching power and mobility in the highest degree, and that in conditions where the front is broken and the battle fluid, the danger to them from hostile artillery and anti-tank weapons is far less than it may be in the initial attack.

Mechanized artillery would naturally accompany them and the only debatable point is whether cavalry or lorry borne infantry, or a combination of the two, should follow to occupy, mop-up, and secure communications. It is unlikely that cross-country lorries will be available in sufficient numbers and consequently the choice would seem to depend on the nature of the terrain and the value of the opposing forces.

The key to the problem of converting a " break in " into a " break through " appears to be a highly mobile reserve containing a powerful punch supplied by armoured fighting vehicles and mechanized artillery, with a sufficiency of cavalry or lorry borne infantry and mechanized machine guns to secure successive bases from which the tanks can make a fresh bound. The whole must be under a selected commander and with a proper staff, signals and probably aircraft. The addition of low-flying assault flights as maintained by some foreign countries is also worthy of consideration.

If this is accepted the necessity for an increase in tanks is obvious, unless we are to forgo their assistance in all the preliminary operations.

There is one possible danger in placing reliance entirely on tanks and that is the possibility that the rifle bullet of the near future may be able to penetrate the armour of all but the heaviest machines.

Accounts of rifles producing muzzle velocities previously undreamt of have appeared in the press. This subject is one on which we have no information but obviously it is of capital importance both to infantry and tanks.

In conclusion, we think that the successive stages of an attack should receive more attention during training that is at present the case, which would include the rapid issue of the shortest orders or instructions based on the situation created by the earlier stages of the attack.

(d) The condition of his own troops as affecting the decision of a commander. (F.S.R., II, Sec. 64 (13) and (14); Sec. 74 (14).)

The question as to whether to press, with or without fresh troops, an attack which has been partially stopped, is one of the most difficult which a commander can have to decide.

History in the past has glorified the commander who has persisted until the last atom of strength has been expended and has thereby snatched victory from defeat. This is sometimes called the " will to win ".

The late war is not devoid of examples of " might have beens " of this nature, but as a general rule our reading of the Official Histories indicates with almost unrelieved monotony that persistence in an attack with tired and weakened units has been a failure, and that piling up infantry has merely meant piling up casualties. Generally speaking an operation which has once failed will not succeed without the introduction of a new factor, and that factor is seldom more infantry. As Brigadier McCulloch states—" In previous times pouring in more riflemen may have been evidence of perseverance and determination on the leaders part. Today it is an indication that the leader does not know his trade ".

The practical points which emerge as regards training are:—

(i) The usual one that the answer to most tactical problems is " more covering fire " and hardly ever " more infantry ".

(ii) That " fresh " as opposed to " more " infantry may be necessary and therefore more attention should be paid by umpires to the probable condition of troops who have already been engaged;

(iii) That troops committed to a certain rôle, such as leap frogging, before operations commence, have ceased to be a reserve to meet a new situation;

(iv) That the employment of reserves is the only way in which a commander can really influence the battle in modern conditions, and that without them he has ceased to be a commander.

12. THE VALUE OF GROUND. (F.S.R., II (Sec. 62 (4).)

In the " gaining of contact " phase we are invited to attack tactical features " which are likely to be the most strongly defended " and this principle is frequently interpreted into attacking the highest ground on all occasions. Such ground is usually earmarked by the defenders as vital to the defence, and the complete elimination of the element of surprise naturally follows. This paragraph of F.S.R. requires revision as the principle of attempting to gain prominent and strongly defended features is, under modern conditions, generally a fallacy.

In the war, particularly on the Western Front, there was a tendency to hold all ground gained however unfavourably situated for defence. This was due to the prevailing offensive policy, and the consequent necessity of keeping as close up as possible to the enemy, to be ready for the next forward move.

It is suggested, however, that the better method would have been to withdraw to a more suitable and salubrious locality, whilst piqueting the enemy's front with advanced troops— a system adopted by the Third Army in June, 1918, when, however, the policy was defensive.

The objection of course is that the forward move of the artillery prior to an attack would be more noticeable, and this has to be balanced against the grave effect on health and casualties of remaining in positions for long periods where every advantage rests with the enemy.

After the first battle of Gaza we wisely fell back with no serious disadvantage to subsequent offensives.

The principle is correctly stated in F.S.R., II, Sec. 64 (14). The Germans invariably adopted it, given time, but their big offensives in 1918 sometimes left them in very uncomfortable positions, notably in the Lys salient, and for precisely the same reasons.

13. COUNTER-ATTACKS.

The history of the war teems with instances of counter-attacks being ordered by higher commanders who had no conception of the actual state of affairs in the front line.

A number of reports by members of the Committee deal with this difficult question, all tending to show that F.S.R., Vol. II, Sec. 82, and to a lesser degree Infantry Training, Vol. II, Sec. 26, are not wholly satisfactory.

These manuals do not emphasize sufficiently clearly—

    (i) The object of the counter-attack.
    (ii) The conditions in which this object can be successfully achieved.
    (iii) The essential differences between the immediate and deliberate counter-attack.

The objects of the counter-attack are—

    (a) To recover ground vital to the defence.
    (b) To close gaps in the defence.
    (c) To exploit an opportunity of dealing the enemy a blow in conditions most advantageous to the defence.

The conditions in which these objects can be successfully achieved.

A study of the numerous counter-attacks delivered in the war lead to the conclusion that the essential factor for success is *surprise*.

Surprise may be achieved in a variety of ways according to the situation, ground, enemy value and methods. In one case the opportunity for surprise may be found in immediate execution, in another by skilful use of ground, in a third by deliberate preparation.

The essential difference between the immediate and deliberate counter-attack.

The immediate counter-attack is nothing more than a platoon or company affair, its object being to stabilize the situation on the defensive front with the aid of the supporting fire immediately available. This object will usually best be served by recapturing the ground lost, but where the losses likely to be incurred therein would endanger the stabilization of the situation, it is this latter which must carry most weight.

The re-establishment of a new defensive front and the recapture of ground vital to the defence are effected by the deliberate counter-attack which is a matter for reserve formations, all arms being concerned. Its object is to restore the situation by the offensive action of all available arms after due preparation, which may be a matter of hours or of days.

The principle that a counter-attack should be made automatically whenever ground was lost, proved more and more costly on the Western Front as the number of machine guns increased, and reinforces the argument that unless the element of surprise is present in some form the counter-attack has no more chance of success against troops in position than any other unprepared and unco-ordinated assault.

14. COUNTER-OFFENSIVES. (F.S.R., II, Sec. 82 (4) and 25 (3).)

The value of this form of operation is often lost sight of in peace training, though some of the greatest British successes—Waterloo, Salamanca—have been fought on this model; the Marne, Tannenberg, Soissons, Romani, and General Chetwode's counter-stroke with the Tenth Division on 27th December, 1917, were examples during the late war.

The great holding power of machine guns makes the defensive stages comparatively easy, but the same factor operates against the decisive counter-stroke on which success depends. We thus come back to the requirements previously discussed for a " break in " and " break through " (para. 11), even when acting on the defensive if, as is usual, there is any intention of an ultimate counter-stroke.

15. ORDERS.

As a result of studying the lessons of the war the principal points in connection with orders against which criticism is directed are the want of : —

(a) Clearness as to the intention of the commander.

(b) Time to enable the order to reach the troops concerned and be acted upon.

(c) Information as to the possibility or otherwise of executing the order.

These failures stand out most prominently in the early and more mobile stages of the war, but they appeared in the subsequent stages of most battles.

The comparatively static nature of the majority of the operations later on led to initial orders becoming increasingly long, intricate and meticulous. This was due in part to the time available for preparation, to distrust of the initiative and tactical ability of subordinate commanders and troops of the new armies, and, lastly, as a precautionary measure against any subsequent official inquiry. The French were equal offenders in this respect, attaching greater importance to the order, as an order, than to its effect on the troops.

These characteristics have been inclined to persist, and the military pendulum appears to have swung too far in the direction of the perfect order, which is in danger of becoming a master rather than a servant.

One difficulty is that in peace exercises without troops, where several syndicates are concerned, the written order is usually the most convenient method of finding out exactly what the commander's plans and arrangements are.

Another and more serious difficulty in all operations is that the subordinate commander seldom disposes of the necessary means for providing sufficient covering fire to carry on independently, because the proportion available in the division is so totally inadequate. So soon as he has to appeal to higher authority for help, centralized control and complicated orders naturally ensue. The fire plan is the forcing house of the voluminous order. The ideal is that a commander should be able to carry on with his own resources on simple verbal orders or instructions containing the superior's object and general plan, until a change in the general situation again requires the intervention of higher authority on broad lines. To realize this ideal his resources in covering fire weapons must be adequate to the task given him, and this is where we fall down at present.

But having stated the difficulties we think that a move might be made in the required direction, and we agree with Major-Generals Fisher and Armitage who put the case as follows : —

" The more rigid the type of warfare, the more formal and precise can orders be.

In mobile operations, however, precise orders cannot be issued to meet every possibility, and commanders will have to act on general instructions. All commanders should, therefore, be trained to work at times on instructions, and not to rigid orders.

The whole tendency of our manuals and teaching since the war has been to lay too much stress on the importance of orders as such. F.S.R., II, Chap. XII, glorifies the precise and formal written order. Operation instructions are only treated as personal and exceptional and the necessity for the frequent issue of brief verbal orders or instructions is hardly dealt with.

The result of this teaching is that many officers are apt to be misled into thinking that, once a written order has been issued, everything will work out satisfactorily. Nothing could be more dangerous or further from the truth.

F.S.R., II, Chap. XII, should be rewritten on broader lines, and sanction should be given to the more general issue of instructions instead of orders, and to the use of verbal orders confirmed in writing when time permits.

It is very desirable that staff officers should be taught to write perfect orders. It is most undesirable that commanders should have their hands tied by formalism in this matter.''

16. DEMOLITIONS.

The Germans were the first to appreciate the efficacy of demolitions as a means of gaining the time required to effect a re-grouping of forces. They used this method to delay the Russians in October, 1914, until their counter-stroke was ready. Again in March, 1917, the Germans had recourse to retirement behind a devastated area; and in their final retreat, they reduced to three brigades the strength of the force which could pursue them on each army front owing to the difficulties of maintenance caused by destruction of communications.

By contrast, the French and Belgian demolitions in 1914 were quite inadequate.

In future, demolition smust be expected to take a prominent place in operations of war.

17. TRAINING MANUALS.

Continental critics in pre-war days used to say that the British Army had the best training manuals and made the worst use of them. Our examination has not led us to question seriously the first part of that criticism. Attention has, however, been drawn by various members of the Committee to points where clarification of F.S.R., II, might be of advantage.

Some of these points have already been discussed and they are included in the following summary only for ease of reference : —

(a) Detachments—para. 16.
(b) Surprise—para. 9.
(c) Counter-attacks—para. 13.
(d) Orders and instructions—para. 15.
(e) A first essential for a retreat is the allotment of roads and the clearing of these roads of transport and impedimenta.

As regards (*e*), efforts were in fact made by G.H.Q. to arrange for parking civilian transport off the roads during the retreat from Mons, but they proved inadequate. Traffic control was then only in its infancy and the resources at the disposal of G.H.Q. were negligible.

The allotment of roads is of course vital, and though this was done within the British Force, less success was achieved as between ourselves and our allies.

Neither point is mentioned in F.S.R., II, Sec. 96. Sec. 41, dealing with the duties of an advanced guard to a retreating force refers to the " clearing away of obstacles " by engineers; Sec. 112, " Marches," does not allude to the question of civilian transport. The subject is only touched on in Sec. 54 (6), dealing with protection.

In peace training the matter is simplified by notices in the press and by the R.A.C. and A.A. organizations. The taking over of these " en bloc " in war might be worthy of consideration.

> (*f*) *Liaison forward.*—F.S.R., II, Sec. 139. The importance of this principle has been indicated in para. 11.

> (*g*) *Covering troops in defence in open warfare.*—F.S.R., II, Sec. 60 (3) and Sec. 62 (1) contemplate that the enemy may use this method, but Sec. 78 (8) discourages the idea of advanced detachments; Sec. 80 (3) does mention the idea of deceiving the enemy but not very robustly, while Sec. 80 (5) considers only protection and warning; though the section adds that they may have to resist and break up the enemy's attack, the general impression conveyed does not bring out sufficiently strongly their use as a definite device to secure surprise. *See* para. 9.

> (*h*) *Counter-attacks.*—F.S.R., II, Sec. 82. *See* para. 13.

> (*i*) *Counter-offensives.*—F.S.R., II, Sec. 82 (4), and 25. The possibility of purposely drawing the enemy forward so that he may be attacked by an indirect line of approach is not mentioned. The third sub-para. on page 43 of F.S.R., II, tends to discourage it. The manœuvre requires a high standard of training, and should be practised in peace time. *See* para. 14.

> (*j*) *Continuation of the attack after the initial phase.*—F.S.R., II, Sec. 75 (i) dealing with this phase refers us back to Sec. 62, which places the onus mainly on the infantry for fighting its way forward with its own weapons in default of other support.

This is the method of infiltration taugh by Ludendorf and it demands a high standard of training and skill in the use of ground. Our infantry possessed it to a high degree in 1914, but there were far fewer machine guns. F.S.R., Sec. 64 (7) tends to discourage this form of operation, by saying that "touch must be maintained with neighbouring units ". Although the next sentence goes on to contradict this thesis, it has both in peace and war frequently been used as a justification for not going forward because troops on the flanks were hung up.

The creation of salients into the enemy's position is the first stage in any successful attack, whether large or small and should be welcomed as such.

All the experiences of the war tend to discount the prospects of gaining any rapid and complete success by methods in which infantry on foot play the chief rôle. Sec. 64 (6) does indeed contemplate the co-operation of artillery and tanks, but utters a warning against expecting too much from them.

In Sec. 61 (2) we find some support for the view previously put forward in this report as to the real solution—

" If the attack penetrates to great depth, some delay may be necessary in order to provide suitable support for the attacking infantry. The action of tanks assisted by smoke may solve this problem and enable the infantry to progress against rear defences."

But even here the remainder of the paragraph indicates that the infantry is still regarded as the predominant arm.

Sec. 75 (2) dealing with the final phases, eventually commits itself to the following opinion: —

" if they have not already been engaged, the action of armoured units at this stage of the battle will have a far reaching effect."

This we believe to be the answer, but we would not limit the action of armoured mobile formations to the final stages since we fear that by the other methods described these phases may never be reached.

This brief summary will we think support our view that the weakest part of F.S.R., II, is its description of the battle after the initial " break in "; what Major-General Kennedy calls the " broken battle—the battle itself ". And this is natural because we have no successful examples on which to go. We are still groping in the dark.

Brigadier McCulloch suggests that tactical operations at training should be allowed to become confused to see what commanders do. Usually the " CEASE FIRE " is sounded, instead of which we should only sound the " STAND FAST ". The object is to prevent peace battles going so quickly that no chance is given for information to find its way back or control to be asserted. As soon as the director sees that commanders have got a reasonable amount of information on which to assert control by making a plan, he should sound the " CONTINUE ".

> (k) *Raids.*—F.S.R., II, Sec. 90 (4); I.T., II, Sec. 18 (2). Major-General McNamara, who has specially studied this subject, concludes that " they are only justifiable as a definite military operation for a specific purpose conducing to the success of commander's plan. They have no place in the conduct of war when carried out merely as a sort of competition between formations with no specific military object. When needlessly ordered they impair the confidence of the troops in their leaders and lower their morale."

In Palestine they were held to be of value in training the raw Indian troops, a point of view which may also have appealed to the Americans. As an operation of war— apart from training—we agree with Major-General McNamara.

On an entirely different footing is the raid in open warfare by armoured fighting vehicles round the enemy's flanks against the rearwards services.

> (l) *Attacking the strongest part of the enemy's position.*— F.S.R., II, Sec. 62 (4). *See* para. 12.
>
> (m) *Consolidation.*—If our reading of history on the subject of counter-attacks (para. 13) and the predominating influence of the machine gun in defence are correct, we appear to make too heavy weather over " consolidation " with a consequent danger of losing opportunities to exploit success. The distribution of the anti-tank weapons and the greatly increased number of machine guns arranged in depth should usually be sufficient security against immediate counter-attack.
>
> Troops should of course be reorganized, but the term " strengthening localities " used in F.S.R., II, Sec. 64 (11) and " measures for consolidation " in Infantry Training, Vol. II, Sec. 11 (31), as interpreted by Sec. 17, are normally taken to mean far more than this.
>
> (n) *The point of attack should be selected to suit the artillery, if the success of the operation depends on its co-operation, and time is of importance.*

F.S.R., II, Sec. 61 (3), 65 and 66 do not mention this principle, while 64 (3) does so very half-heartedly.

It raises a most important question—*see* alternative (a) of para. 10.

C.—EQUIPMENT AND ORGANIZATION

18. ARTILLERY AMMUNITION.

We are agreed that shrapnel ought to be abolished in order to simplify training in peace and shooting in war, as well as the manufacture and supply of ammunition in the field.

We are reinforced in our opinion by enemy experience.[*] The German combined shrapnel and H.E. shell was a failure. The field artillery of the Allies proved superior and our H.E. shell was particularly unpleasant. Our shrapnel had some effect on occasions, but in general was not particularly formidable. The Austrians continued to use shrapnel for a long time, but eventually abandoned it. We find the same difficulties as the Germans in attempting to use shrapnel for predicted shooting for which it is unsuitable. Apart from this, complications must arise in war from the multiplicity of types of ammunition in the field.

We are impressed by the necessity for the introduction of H.E. shell as the principal field gun projectile. We fully realize the present difficulties of adoption, due chiefly to the facts that the 18-pr. was designed as a shrapnel gun and that its H.E. shell with direct action fuze is not ideal and requires improvement.

We consider that as a matter of policy the General Staff should lay down that H.E. shell is to be the principal field gun projectile and that the question should be studied in detail by the expert authorities concerned, with the object of abolishing shrapnel at the first available opportunity.

19. GUNS AND HOWITZERS.

If shrapnel is abandoned the balance of argument appears guns, more particularly so if the firing of barrages in mobile guns, more particularly so if the firing of barracks in mobile warfare as a normal method of support is not feasible.

The chief argument in the contrary sense is the superiority of the gun against tanks, but we regard the provision of a far lighter and more mobile anti-tank weapon as axiomatic.

20. MEDIUM AND HEAVY ARTILLERY.

The moral and material effect of the German 5·9-in. howitzer shell in 1914 will not have been forgotten by any who experienced it, and this was merely the beginning.

The increasing weight of weapon which mechanical traction enables armies to maintain in the field in modern conditions is one of the main lessons of the war.

---

[*] " Die Deutsche Artillerie in den Durchsbruchschlachten des Weltkrieges (Bruchmuller) (1922 edition), pages 14-16."

21. LIGHTENING THE EQUIPMENT CARRIED BY THE INFANTRY SOLDIER.

That this is necessary is our unanimous opinion. An exhausted soldier is only half a soldier, and the Official Histories show that our standard of man-management in the war fell considerably behind that of our horse-management.

The British citizen walks less and less in peace, and the effect on his marching powers in war must not be lost sight of.

We may train our regular army to a fairly high standard, but in the main we must legislate for the town-bred recruit. We believe the matter is now receiving the attention of the Army Council, and we need say no more.

22. SIMPLIFYING THE WEAPONS IN THE INFANTRY BATTALION.

Into this thorny question we do not propose to enter, since it is being studied by those better qualified to do so. At present we can with great difficulty and at the expense of the rifle companies train the required number of specialists in several years of peace, but whether we can keep them up in war is quite another question.

Foreign armies are able, in peace as in war, to organize heavy machine guns, trench mortars and so on into regimental units serving three battalions, a plan which we also found it necessary to adopt in the late war.

We, on the other hand, have been forced since 1918, by our peace distribution, to incorporate supporting arms in each battalion and this greatly complicates our problem.

Until this difficulty can be overcome, any solution is bound to be a compromise and, as such, unsatisfactory. But, as stated in para. 10 (alternative (d)) we think this main difficulty is not insoluble. In any case we suggest that the first essential is to have a clear view as to what the future rôle of the infantry battalion in war is to be, and then to go as near as we can to it in the matter of equipment, without unfitting units for their normal duties in obligatory garrisons.

The real point is whether infantry battalions are to be required to fight their way forward with their own weapons, in which case commanders naturally require their own supporting arms, or whether they are to be considered as one component, the remainder being supplied from outside the battalion.

The Official Histories show that the former method was gradually abandoned in favour of the latter.

23. THE ENTRENCHING TOOL.

There is no question but that in any future war, as in the late war, troops will have to dig.

Evidence as to the value of the entrenching tool is, however, conflicting. On the Western Front during the mobile phases it was most valuable; in Gallipoli it could not compete with the root-entangled ground; as to Palestine and Mesopotamia we have no evidence; on the Indian frontier it would be useless.

In our opinion, as we must lighten the equipment of the infantry soldier, this tool should be carried like other tools on transport under centralized control. It would then be issued when required for any specific operation.

But so soon as this system is adopted we think it probable that the need for a light tool would disappear, because no one who really anticipated having to dig seriously would be content with such an inefficient implement if he could get bigger and better one. This was the general experience in the war.

24. INTERCOMMUNICATION.

In para. 11 (b), we advocate the substitution of wireless for cable in front of brigade headquarters, with the possible exception of artillery lines. We do not mean this to imply that the development of wireless for artillery is not desirable. On the contrary, it is, in our opinion, essential to that arm, and present experiments in that direction should be pressed forward. But we advocate the retention of cable for artillery, which in certain conditions would otherwise lose in efficiency.

25. THE NECESSITY FOR A COMPREHENSIVE REVIEW OF THE PROPORTION AMONG THE VARIOUS ARMS.

In the foregoing paragraphs we have dealt with a few points of comparative detail on which the Official Histories of the War shed some light. In doing so we have merely touched the fringe of the real problems in connection with organization and equipment, as affecting preparation for war in the future.

No war is like the one which precedes it, and it is quite obvious that this will be so in the case which we are now considering. During the mobile period of the war in the West, many of the weapons which figured in the later stages existed only in small quantities or were absent altogether. In Eastern Theatres during the mobile stages the Turk was a second-class soldier with barely a second-class equipment according to present day standards.

From these Eastern Campaigns we may derive some lessons for what Training Memorandum, No. 4A, styles " The average condition ". Except in the matter of degree they furnish no exception to the general conclusion which emerges from all the campaigns which we have studied, viz., that the present proportion between arms covering and arms covered does not conform to the lessons of the war, in so far as offensive operations are concerned.

Looking back at the constantly increasing number of covering weapons which was found necessary as the war proceeded, it is clear that a return to practically a pre-war standard in such weapons cannot be reconciled with the ever-growing numbers of machine guns likely to be encountered by the " major expedition " against a second-class or even a third-class enemy.

The Japanese have recently demonstrated this patent fact in the operations near Shanghai. It is true that the conditions there which cramped manœuvre were not favourable to the more highly trained and equipped army. Manœuvre, leading to an indirect approach and tactical surprise, may sometimes suffice to restore the balance of advantage in our favour, but history shows that we cannot place complete reliance on these factors, however much we should strive to achieve them. More often have adverse conditions—mountain or desert, marshes or want of water—forced us to operate on well-marked and obvious lines of approach ending in direct attack. The holding power of automatic weapons favours us only in those localities where we can stand strictly on the defensive.

Unfortunately, we know from past experience that, like every other policeman, we may often be forced to act offensively, tactically if not strategically. The General Staff appears to envisage such action in what it considers to be the " average condition ". Our training manuals stress the principle of offensive action, but if the lessons of the War are any guide to the future it is very doubtful whether we are organized and equipped to carry out their precepts.

What is the solution ?

The enemy is the primary factor on which everything else depends. In 1914 we were quite clear on this point and our war preparations, so far as our small regular Army permitted, attained in consequence a standard probably unequalled in the history of the British Army.

If we were unduly optimistic as to the effect which that small Army would produce in a struggle between nations in arms, it was no fault of the Army authorities who, as now, had to make the best of what they could get after providing for obligatory garrisons overseas.

Army Training Memorandum, No. 4A, of 1932, shows that at present the enemy cannot be defined, and this absence of a basis to the problem adds enormously to the difficulties of its solution. This being the case, it appears necessary to fall back on to a tentative method of procedure in the direction which the lessons of the War indicate as most generally desirable.

The chief lesson is the necessity for increased covering fire to make movement over a bullet and shell swept area in any way possible, this applies primarily to movement by unarmoured men, but that it will also be applicable to armoured fighting vehicles appears likely from the analogy of the gun ashore and the gun afloat, where the fixed platform has the advantage.

It seems that we should not be wrong in expanding our resources in tanks to clear the way for the infantry, whether on foot or motorized, and that we may also require more artillery to protect both, though this is less certain in the case of a major expedition. These measures appear to be suitable to all our war problems, with the exception of minor operations in difficult country, for which specially organized forces may be necessary. And this adaptability is important because behind the major expedition lies the shadow of the national war. If this contingency is remote, it is nevertheless vital and can never be lost sight of.*

Indeed it may well seem less remote than it was when these Training Memoranda were issued. It looks as if the holders of all the trophies might in due course be called upon to defend their titles.

Relieved of restrictions, the Germans are likely to go in largely for tanks, since their few war experiences with these weapons were most encouraging† and their industrial strength favours war in the workshop. With this aim in the background the Russian Government are also endeavouring to industrialize their country.

Should we again have to intervene on the Continent we must be prepared for mobile warfare supported by every possible mechanical or scientific contrivance, on or over the ground.

All present indications show that in such a war the armoured fighting vehicle will play a prominent part, for we are by no means the only country which is thinking in terms of mobility and armour, though at the moment we have made more progress than most others.

To sum up, the problem is to increase the proportion of tanks certainly, artillery probably and other covering weapons possibly, and this without increasing the size of the division, which would unfit it for the " average condition ".

In the case of the individual soldier, our reading of history leads us to believe that the equipment which he carries must be reduced to what he always requires and that anything else must be carried for him and issued to him as and when necessary. Mechanical transport enables this to be done without undue risk.

---

* Training Memorandum No. 4A, 1932, para. 9.
† " Der Stellungskrieg," Part 7, by Friederich Seeselberg.

We have suggested (para. 10 (*d*)) that this same principle might be followed in order to simplyfy the infantry battalion, *i.e.*, that some of the complications should be drawn back into a divisional unit, from which they could be distributed, complete with personnel, as and when required. Here again, mechanization should help us. We would like to see the same elastic organization carried further to include our larger formations. This would mean a comparatively simple and preferably smaller Division, to which could be added as required those extra units, tanks, field, medium and heavy artillery, aircraft, etc., as appear most suitable to meet the conditions of the particular operations in question. In other words, we advocate a handier standard formation and an increase in corps or army covering-fire weapons, and this we believe to be the teaching of the War as applied to present day problems. How is this to be done?

We have made the definite suggestion to convert a proportion of the infantry battalions in divisions into combined machine gun and anti-tank units and possibly mortar units.

As regards additional tanks, we think that the line of least resistance might be to re-arm other infantry battalions with armoured fighting vehicles, and this may eventually lead to infantry brigades being reduced from 4 to 3 battalions. We should thus get a smaller and handier division, with much more " punch " behind it for mobile warfare.

We have already mentioned the objections to small corps, which are a handicap to re-organization owing to difficulties in equalizing promotion when one is expanded at another's expense. There is also the cost in peace of a complete hierarchy and complications on mobilization.

These converted battalions should therefore remain in the infantry fold as " armoured infantry," leaving the position of the existing battalions of the Royal Tank Corps for later consideration.

We may eventually arrive at a solution when we shall have armoured units in each of the three main arms—cavalry, artillery and infantry. And here we must leave the matter, for we recognize that to pursue it further would lead us into questions, of which finance is only one which are outside our province.

From a detached and somewhat remote view point, we have indicated what appears to us to be the ideal objective in theory—and a possible method of approach—if we are to. reconcile the sound precepts of our manuals with our ability to carry them out in the light of the lessons of the war.

We appreciate that there are obstacles intervening and to those more competent to assess their nature and importance we must leave the plan of operations.

In conclusion, we would recommend that from the suggested review, the scale of air co-operation should not be excluded.

D.—TRAINING

26. Instructions and Manuals.

These have been dealt with in para. 17 and the general conclusion is that, with a few exceptions, they correctly embody the teaching of the war. It is, indeed, possible to find support in them for almost any action in any combination of circumstances, and therefore the necessary element in a correct choice is common sense. As Major-General McNamara truly says: " With so much advice available there is a danger of the officer seeking the answer to a specific problem from a page in the book rather than from common sense, reinforced by well-digested military knowledge. When he errs, he is apt to lament his folly in having got on to the wrong page rather than to blame his lack of judgement and common sense."

27. Training generally.

The greatest difficulty at the present time in all training with troops is to reconcile the tactics taught in our manuals with the armament of the troops, which has now become unsuitable for carrying them out, owing, as we believe, to a faulty proportion between the arms. There are in addition experiments in process which are obviously necessary, but which tend to discredit many of the methods on which the bulk of the Army is being organized and trained.

These factors lead to difficulties in exercises with troops, particularly for the infantry in the case of attack against a first-class enemy.

The infantry soldier sees the following developments since the war:—

> (a) The multiplication of machine guns and increase in their efficiency, *i.e.,* an increase in the power of defence.
>
> (b) The very considerable reduction in our artillery, *i.e.,* a decrease in the power of attack.
>
> (c) The rapid progress in power and performance of tanks, *i.e.,* a serious threat to infantry both in attack and defence.

There is no lack of verbal encouragement and exhortation to the infantryman to fight his way forward with his own weapons. The infantryman who actually spent the war in an unit is naturally sceptical. From this point of view the latitude given by the most recent amendment to Training and Manœuvre Regulations, permitting operations dealing with a class of enemy, against which infantry with its present armament may hope to operate successfully, is doubtless a relief. In general, however, there is no escaping the difficulties, which are:—

(i) We have no specific war problem as we had before 1914.
(ii) Our organization and equipment are in a state of flux and obviously unsuited to war against a first-class or even a second-class opponent.
(iii) The comparative value to be attached to the different arms is the subject of controversy.

There are, however, certain aspects of training which are quite independent of organization and equipment, and in concentrating on these we cannot go wrong. Physical fitness is one of them. Another is the training of leaders on whom the efficiency of the Army depends; the development of the qualities of common sense, decision and character, as apart from pure knowledge, are the characteristics of a leader. Some of us have been struck by the lack of self-confidence in many senior regimental officers. This indicates a fault in our training. The point is excellently put in the amendment to Training and Manœuvre Regulations referred to above, the kernel of the whole matter being the development of reasoning and not memory.

The wide scope of operations now permissible offers every opportunity for giving that variation in problems which is so necessary to avoid the stereotyped solution and force officers to argue from first principles.

We think, however, that in exercises with troops obvious unrealities should be avoided if possible, and problems be suited to the ground and other local conditions. Conditions in our various garrisons are diverse enough to include in an officer's service almost every aspect of war. The small amount of practice devoted to combined operations, even though many of our stations lack facilities for anything else, show that we do not always make the best use of local training possibilities. One of the lessons of the war was the manner in which the Germans appreciated the realities of any situation and acted accordingly.

As regards exercises, both with and without troops, we feel that the fog of war has frequently been too thin, and that perhaps undue attention has been paid to " How to do " something, rather than to " What to do ".

The influence of air observation has been referred to in para. 9. In this connection we should add that however necessary the training of Royal Air Force observers may be, the training of a few officers who may shortly afterwards be transferred to quite another part of the Air Force has to be balanced against the necessity of training commanders to work for surprise in conditions when it is reasonably possible of achievement. It may be argued that they will have to compete against an observation in war, but in war events move more slowly and there is more time to plan and carry out the initial arrangements, amongst which temporary command of the air over a restricted area may well find a place.

It is suggested that the training of observers might be carried out during exercises without necessarily communicating the full result of their observations to commanders.

Apart from the above generalities, some constructive suggestions have been made by various members of the committee which are summarized below.

28. TRAINING OF SENIOR COMMANDERS.

(*a*) Attention is directed in the various histories to the fact that many commanders were too old for their work, and lacked the necessary physical energy and stamina to withstand the strain of active service conditions.

(*b*) A second point is that officers likely to rise to high command should be given experience in peace-time of conditions in eastern theatres. If this could be combined with giving a larger number of Indian Army officers spells of duty at home, in exchange for an equal number of appointments for British Service officers in India, both services would benefit.

(*c*) Another suggestion is that more practice in command should, if possible, be given to the higher ranks. It is thought that this question requires separate treatment from the normal training envisaged in Training and Manœuvre Regulations.

(*d*) We shall have to enlist the help of officers in the Reserve as in 1914. It would be advantageous if we could do something to keep them up to date, but financially this is probably out of the question at present.

The necessity for keeping senior officers unemployed for considerable periods is doubtless unavoidable, but that they do not usually benefit by such periods of " cold storage " is probably agreed. Would it not be possible to do more to keep them in touch than is done at present? Attachment to commands for the receipt of training pamphlets was a first step in the right direction, but we think that it does not go far enough. The small expenditure of money involved would seem more than justified, but in default of money the acceptance of the principle would be better than nothing.

(*e*) The system of peace brevets, a considerable proportion of which are allotted to officers who have graduated at the Staff College, means that it is from the Staff Colleges that many of our future commanders will come. In selecting students for nominations it is suggested that this point should be kept prominently in view.

29. TRAINING OF OFFICERS IN GENERAL.

Major-General Kennedy puts the crucial questions—" Does our training encourage self-reliance and initiative in subordinate leaders "?

His impression is that there is too much criticism and too little instruction. We feel that there is something in this stricture, and that it may lead to loss of self-confidence and reliance on their own judgment, which in war is often all that officers will have to rely on.

The shortage of men in the infantry makes the question particularly difficult in the case of that arm.

We agree, however, that we must not reduce the proportion of officers maintained in peace-time, in view of the inevitable expansion in time of war.

War histories show that Training and Manœuvre Regulations are correct in stating that " the efficiency of an army depends on the efficiency of its leaders ".

30. TRAINING OF THE RANK AND FILE.

The fundamental question on which everything else depends is that of the rôle of the Regular Army.

Training and Manœuvre Regulations state that " it is important to recognize the great expansion of our existing forces which a national war would demand ". We have suggested in para. 4 that considerable expansion will be necessary in any war and, if this is so, we ought to try and produce from our Regular Army the highest proportion possible of junior leaders. But in our peace training, we are apt to lose sight of this and to keep on raising the standard of the small regular nucleus in directions which do not produce the leader, and to a pitch which is unattainable by war-trained recruits.

From this point of view, simplification in the arms and equipment of the infantry battalion is a matter of primary importance, for, as things are at present, infantry, which used to be regarded as the simplest arm to train, is fast becoming the most complicated. This point we have already attempted to cover in our proposed machine gun battalion. Another suggested line of investigation is the possibility of simplifying infantry drill. Anything in this direction would tend to simplify the problem of training the war recruit.

Yet another question which we have considered is the balance between weapon training and other forms of training more calculated to produce the leader, and the proportion of time allotted to each. The short discussion possible in the time has shown a marked divergence of opinion on this subject.

One view, which is held by the President and some members, is that the scales are at present unduly weighted in favour of shooting on the range. The reasons are given in the Report on Gallipoli, and the difficulties of making practical suggestions for cutting down the time spent on shooting are fully admitted. The number of rounds fired by the trained soldier has already been reduced, and some think the remedy worse than the disease owing to the resulting complications in the programme. But those who hold that too much time out of the collective training period is devoted to shooting would go further and eliminate all elements of competition, either for battalion averages or pay. Other members of the Committee think these proposals most undesirable. They hold firmly to the principle that ability to shoot straight is the first and most important duty of the infantry soldier and that this must not be sacrificed to anything else.

Some minor ways in which the number of days spent on the range might be reduced have been suggested, such as, increase in range facilities, ability to obtain the services of range wardens whenever required, and discretion to fire a greater number of rounds per man per day than is at present permissible, but they only touch the fringe of the problem.

Though we are divided on the question of the weapon training course, there is a consensus of opinion that the greatest obstacles of all to the training of the present day infantry soldier are the weakness of effectives, combined with the fact that practically all fatigue and routine duties fall on this arm. The usual suggestion of Employment Companies in peace-time has been made to overcome this latter difficulty, but we are agreed that if money were available for such companies it would be better expended on bringing battalions up to their peace establishments.

We understand that the question of extending the cycle of training, is already under investigation by the War Office.

In conclusion we would like to repeat that the object of all our training should be to produce the maximum number of potential junior leaders, and not the individual expert.

31. THE TERRITORIAL ARMY.

The definite acceptance of the principle that the Territorial Army will form the sole basis for the expansion of the Regular Army in war, and the administrative steps taken to implement this decision, should mark an advance as compared with our position in 1914.

The decision then taken on mobilization by Lord Kitchener to start a parallel and competitive organization in the form of the New Army cut across such measures as were in existence to mobilize and train the Territorial Army, hampered as the War Office already was by the absence of any obligation by the Territorials to serve overseas. All the new formations displayed the weaknesses which might have been expected.

On the Western front they stepped straight into position warfare, where neither quick thinking nor quick decisions were required, and in these conditions they were fairly efficient; but mobile operations of any kind immediately revealed their limitations. These were particularly noticeable at the Suvla Bay landing, where they naturally failed in conditions which would have severely tried Regular troops.

The limitations of war-trained troops were not confined to ourselves, but were shown by the armies of all the combatants in all theatres. Only by the specialized training of specially selected men during the winter 1917-18 did the Germans temporarily overcome them in the spring and summer of 1918.

Judging from the war, it would seem that the high average level of intelligence in Territorial units enabled them to reach a fair standard in a restricted syllabus, but the moment operations moved outside that syllabus, they had nothing to fall back upon. The Regular, as he moves about the world, is constantly faced with fresh problems, and his far wider experience in peace enables him to draw on latent stores of accumulated military knowledge to meet the unforeseen in war. It would be a sad commentary on our long service training if this were not so. Conditions in the wide open spaces of some of our Dominions tend also to develop resource in the face of unexpected conditions which is so essential for the soldier.

These are the facts. It remains to consider to what extent they can be overcome in training during peace and after the outbreak of war.

As regards peace, although the Territorial Army now accepts the obligation to serve overseas, the limitations of peace training which we fear are insuperable, the weakness of effectives, and the probability that a proportion will not be fit for general service, will in combination mean that a considerable number of war-raised recruits will be required to complete every unit to war establishment, unless we break up some units to complete others—which would, psychologically, be unfortunate.

Possibly the most valuable part of the Territorial Army is the provision of the framework on to which the necessary effectives can be grafted.

In peace-time the men actually serving provide a means of training the cadres in duties of command, and in this connection we agree with the policy which aims at tightening the bonds between Territorials and Regulars.

Though it may interfere with the training of the latter, we think that this is more than compensated for by the opportunities offered to Regular officers and non-commissioned officers for supervising the training of men, of which the existing weakness of their own units might otherwise deprive them. Those who thus do a period of training with Territorial units return with added confidence and an increased sense of responsibility.

To come back to the problem of achieving the highest possible standard for units largely recruited after the outbreak of war, the infiltration of Regular personnel into the " Kitchener " Divisions does not seem to have been as efficacious as it ought to have been; but it must be remembered that, for various reasons, many of the officers infiltrated were available only because they had not been considered fit for retention in or promotion to the very Commands in peace to which they were posted in the New Armies for war. As a fact they did produce good results.

We think that the infiltration of Regular personnel is the only possible solution, but since conditions must be more difficult in the Territorial than in the Regular unit, the best officers and non-commissioned officers must be selected.

In the war we set our faces against special assault divisions. As a general principle we ought to try and avoid any marked difference in the standard of efficiency of our units and formations. This means the greatest possible amalgamation of Regulars and Territorials which the circumstances permit. How far this is possible, however, depends on the rôle of the Regular Army, which may be:—

(a) A spearhead;
(b) A covering force to gain time;
(c) A nucleus for expansion to a larger or even to a National Army.

In the choice, unfortunately, we may not be free agents as was the case in 1914 when the Regular Army was practically expended on (a) and (b), and what was left for (c) consisted only of stragglers brought from stations overseas, or when we had to resort to such desperate expedients for training the New Armies as the employment of pensioners, officers of cadet battalions and old soldiers from reserve battalions and other second-class material.

We should try and do better than this in a future emergency, even at the expense of some loss of efficiency in the Regular formations.

Our first suggestion is that arrangements should be made for the transfer of a definite proportion of Regular personnel, preferably in the middle and junior ranks of officers and non-commissioned officers, to all units of the Territorial Army. The ideal would be to transfer an equal number of corresponding ranks from the Territorial Army to the Regular Army. We realize, however, that the pledge to the Territorial Army introduces an element of uncertainty into the latter part of the proposals. Should the required number not be forthcoming, the vacancies would have to be filled from other sources. If Regular units are available from amongst those moving overseas at a later date, they might be used to train alongside the Territorial Army units, but as stated above, this depends on the mobilization requirements for the spearhead or covering force.

Our second suggestion is that, recognizing the limitations of peace training for the Territorial soldier, and the impossibility after mobilization of having sufficient time to attain to the normal standard of the Regulars, a syllabus should be drawn up for each arm, limited in scope to what it is most essential to learn. This would vary from time to time according to the most probable campaign.

32. CONCLUSION.

On the subject of training it is possible to write interminably. In concluding we cannot do better than quote Major-General McNamara—

" In looking back at the war and all its lessons we must not overlook the most important lesson of all, viz., all wars produce new methods and fresh problems. The last war was full of surprises—the next one is likely to be no less prolific in unexpected developments. Hence we must study the past in the light of the probabilities of the future, which is what really matters. No matter how prophetic we may be, the next war will probably take a shape far different to our peace-time conceptions.

In order to cope with this upset to our preconceived ideas our leaders must be versatile, mentally robust and full of common sense and self-reliance.

To produce this sort of mentality must be the object of our training."

W. KIRKE, *Lieut.-General,*
President.

C. C. ARMITAGE, *Major-General.*

A. W. BARTHOLOMEW, *Major-General.*

B. D. FISHER, *Major-General.*

R. G. H. HOWARD-VYSE, *Brigadier.*

J. KENNEDY, *Major-General.*

A. J. McCULLOCH, *Brigadier.*

A. E. McNAMARA, *Major-General.*

A. R. SELBY, *Major,*
Secretary.

THE WAR OFFICE,
13*th October*, 1931.

B40/95) 500 3/40 W.O.P. 4651

REPORT OF THE COMMITTEE

ON THE

LESSONS OF THE GREAT WAR

APPENDICES

THE WAR OFFICE,
October, 1932.

(A 3629—Appendices)

REPORT OF THE COMMITTEE

ON THE

LESSONS OF THE GREAT WAR

APPENDICES

THE WAR OFFICE,
October, 1932.

(A 3629—Appendices)

CONTENTS

APPENDIX I

REPORT ON THE LESSONS OF THE GREAT WAR ON THE WESTERN FRONT BY MAJOR-GENERAL A. E. McNAMARA, C.B., C.M.G., D.S.O.

References quoted are to the History of the Great War, Military Operations, France and Belgium, Vols. I to V.

ARRANGEMENT OF REPORT

PART I.—Readiness for War.
PART II.—Tactical Lessons.
PART III.—Organization and Equipment.
PART IV.—Administration.
PART V.—Training.

PART I.—READINESS FOR WAR

General.—The price paid for lack of war preparation needs no elaboration. Some of the more important lessons are indicated below.

1. *Mobilization of the expeditionary force.*—A first essential on the outbreak of war is the capacity to mobilize at once our expeditionary force, complete in every detail, and to transport it overseas.

1914 provides a lesson how to do this.

2. *The War Office staff.*—The War Office staff must remain unchanged to conduct the war. In 1914 nearly everyone who mattered at once proceeded overseas, with unfortunate results in the conduct of the war.

3. *Territorial Army.*—Complete schemes for the mobilization of the Territorial Army must be in existence, and resources in Regular Instructors, equipment, camping grounds and training areas available for their training.

4. *Reinforcements.*—Machinery should be immediately available for receiving and training reinforcements.

In 1914 the Special Reserve carried out this rôle.

Under present arrangements its place is to be taken by training cadres to be formed on mobilization.

Are we convinced that the necessary staff of instructors, especially in all specialist subjects, is at once available? This is vital.

In this connection it is to be noted that in the late war it was found necessary to form a machine gun corps in order to train machine gun reinforcements. We have now far more machine guns and the subject is much more complicated.

Can the training battalions deal with it?

5. *Army Schools.*—Many of these will have to be expanded. Do schemes exist and is the instructional staff available?

6. *Recruiting.*—The late war proves that organization and data must be in existence for maintaining the supply of recruits. This requirement holds good to a greater or less extent whether the war be a major expedition or a National War.

7. *Munitions, equipment and weapons.*—Organization and plant must be in being to provide these in time and in sufficient quantity. Our troubles in this respect in the late war are on record.

8. *Experiments.*—There must be an organization to keep abreast of the development of weapons and devices as an outcome of war experience.

9. *Officers.*—Finally we must have an adequate supply for all purposes of that invaluable article—the Regimental Officer. A study of the war, and indeed of events in peace, forces home the conclusion that the backbone of our Army is the 1914 type of Regimental Officer, with his complement the N.C.O. His influence is immeasurable, whether it be in times of anxiety in peace, in the turmoil of a war, or in the subjugation and administration of huge and little known semi-civilized areas; or as a model for the different grade of officer recruited during a war. No other type will do. The men trust him implicitly—savage countries bow to his rule—the war officers gladly take him as their model. These statements are well borne out by the war. The lesson on war preparation is that economy in our establishment of regular officers in peace is likely to prove costly in war. He is not a luxury, but an insurance, for which the premium is well worth paying.

PART II.—TACTICAL LESSONS

Conduct of the Retreat from Mons

General.—In considering the conduct of the retreat from Mons it is necessary to bear in mind that the C.-in-C. of the British Expeditionary Force was operating under conditions of extreme difficulty owing to the initial misconception of the situation by the French High Command, to the faulty intelligence with which he was provided, and to his difficulty in ascertaining the situation and intention of the French Fifth Army on his right.

Whatever the reason, however, it must be admitted that the conduct of the retreat is open to criticism, and the following remarks are intended to bring to notice points for future guidance.

Lesson 1. (*Location of headquarters*).

" In a retirement the headquarters of all formations should be well forward." (F.S.R., Vol. II, Sec. 96.2.)

Narrative.—On Aug. 23rd, 1914, the B.E.F., on the general line of the Mons canal, successfully held up the advance of the German IX, III and IV Corps (First Army) (Vol. I, pp. 83 and 85). In view of reports from the Fifth French Army the British C.-in-C. decided about midnight on an immediate retirement (Vol. I, p. 84). Senior Staff Officers of Corps were accordingly summoned to G.H.Q. and received verbal orders about 1 a.m., Aug. 24th, for an immediate retreat. Not only was G.H.Q. at Le Cateau, some 35 miles from Corps H.Q., but there was no cable communication with the II Corps H.Q. (Vol. I, p. 88)— Hence the orders for the retirement got out very late to the troops with consequent uncertainty and confusion. (Vol. I, p. 91.) Similar instances of G.H.Q. being too far back, with critical results, occur later in the retreat.

On the night of Aug. 25th G.H.Q. was established at St. Quentin some 25 miles from Corps H.Q. B.E.F. Operation Order No. 8 issued at 7.30 p.m. prescribed the continuance of the retreat on Aug. 26th (Vol. I, p. 133)—Owing to his distance from the scene of operations the C.-in-C. issued these orders without a correct appreciation of the situation of his two corps. In effect they were both in difficulties—neither corps was in a position to carry out the movements indicated in G.H.Q. Operation Order No. 8. The II Corps unsupported fought a decisive action on Aug. 26th at Le Cateau (Vol. I, p. 134) while the I Corps retired away from it on the east of the R. Oise. A gap of some 15 miles was thus created between both corps which was not closed for several days, during which a dangerous situation existed.

Whether the events on Aug. 26th were in our favour, or otherwise, it seems clear that G.H.Q. had little influence on the situation.

Again in the critical situation on the evening of Aug. 26th we find G.H.Q. back at Noyon out of touch with Corps Commanders (Vol. I, p. 192).

We find the same tendency to keep headquarters too far back both in trench warfare operations, and in our retreat in 1918, with consequent loss of control.

Manuals.—F.S.R., Vol. II, Sec. 96 (2) is quite clear as to the importance of H.Q. being well forward in a retreat. The reason given is not, however, complete as the vital importance of Control is not mentioned.

Our Training.—This is sound on the subject.

Lesson 2. (Plans for a withdrawal)

" It is the duty of a commander on the defensive to have a plan prepared for a possible withdrawal." (F.S.R., Vol. II, Sec. 96.1.)

Narrative.—Although it was realized as early as the evening of Aug. 22nd that the contingency of a withdrawal must be faced (Vol. I, p. 59) there is little in the official history to indicate the existence of such a plan, and the somewhat sketchy verbal orders issued at 1 a.m. on Aug. 24th to staff officers of Corps do not point to a well thought out scheme of retirement (Vol. I, p. 88)—It is obvious that if higher formation commanders had been secretly informed of the C.-in-Cs. plan should a retirement become necessary, the task of giving effect to his midnight retreat orders would have been much simplified.

Manuals.—F.S.R., Vol. II, Sec. 96 (1), deals with the requirement of a pre-arranged plan, but seems to try to cover two different problems in one precept. There must be a difference in the method of retirement of a force:—

(*a*) Fighting a delaying action, and
(*b*) A force on the defensive forced to retire by enemy action.

In the first case the ideal should be to slip away before, not after (as stated in F.S.R., Vol. II, 96 (1)) the enemy has captured the position. It is really not quite clear which of the above two rôles G.H.Q. envisaged for the B.E.F. at Mons. There was possibly some confusion of thought, and it is suggested that the wording of F.S.R. is not calculated to clarify matters in the future.

Training.—Our training is sound as far as it goes, but our problems are usually far simpler than those confronting a Commander in war.

Lesson 3. (Clearing roads prior to withdrawal)

" A first essential for a retreat is the allotment of roads, and the clearing of those roads of transport and impediments."

Narrative.—One of the primary causes of our troubles during the retreat was that the march of our columns was constantly blocked by French troops crossing our line of march, refugees and their transport, and our own transport mixed up with the above. One reason for this state of affairs is that no allotment of roads between ourselves and the French was made before the morning of Aug. 26th (Vol. I, p. 114). How the refugees question could have been dealt with is not clear, but one feels that the Germans under similar conditions would have found some solution to the problem. Be this as it may the fact remains that the blocking of roads not only imposed enormous hardship on the troops, and made the conduct of rearguards difficult and precarious, but also had an important bearing on the campaign.

On Aug. 25th the marches of both the I and II Corps were much impeded by French troops and refugees (Vol. I, pp. 114, 115, 117, 118, 120, 127, 142)—One result was that the troops of the II Corps reached the Le Cateau position so late in the evening, so exhausted, and with the Germans so close on their heels, that the corps commander was forced to stand and fight at Le Cateau on Aug. 26th. If the roads had been clear on Aug. 25th there would probably have been no battle on Aug. 26th, and the campaign might have developed differently.

Manuals.—F.S.R., Vol. II, Sec. 96, does not mention either the allotment of roads, or refugees.

Training.—Our training is sound, but our peace time retirements are perhaps made too easy.

Lesson 4. (*Rear guards and rallying positions*)

" Organization of rear guards and the selection of rallying positions enable a retreat to be carried out on methodical lines."

Narrative.—From personal experience in the I Corps, and from a study of the official history as regards the II and III Corps, rear guards seem to have been adequately organized (except perhaps weak in artillery) and rallying positions chosen as far as possible—(Vol. I, pp. 88, 89, 141, 81)—A methodical conduct of the rear guards seems, however, to have been almost impossible owing to the constant and unforeseen checks of the main bodies caused by the roads being blocked as indicated in Lesson 3. A timed programme of withdrawal (F.S.R. II, Sec. 45. 2) was clearly not practicable as an estimate of the rate of progress of the main body was quite impossible. The fate of the infantry of a rear guard was often to be withdrawn from its position and closed, and promptly told to re-occupy it owing to the main body being again stopped. In short the conduct of our rear guards was far removed from our conception of such operations, but the basic cause was the initial error (preventable or otherwise) in not clearing the roads.

Manuals.—F.S.R., Vol. II, Sec. 96. 44 and 45 deal adequately with the subject.

Training.—Our training is sound, but our exercises develop in too orderly a manner and are far removed from the situations which actually occurred in the retreats of 1914 and 1918.

Lesson 5. (*Intercommunications in Rear Guard actions*)

" Reliable intercommunication between the main body and rear guard and between all portions of the rear guard is essential." (F.S.R., Vol. II, Sec. 44. 3.)

Narrative.—The importance of this precept, and the difficulty of giving effect to it, stand out clearly from a perusal of the retreat from Mons. Many regrettable incidents would have been obviated by better communications, *viz.*:—

> Aug. 24th, Mons. 2nd Bn. D.W.R. failed to get the order to retire. Result 400 casualties (Vol. I, p. 99).
>
> Aug. 24th, Mons. Commander Cav. Div. failed with three officers to get touch with II Corps. Hence the division retired prematurely, thereby uncovering left flank of II Corps. (Vol. I, pp. 96 and 99.)
>
> Aug. 24th, Elouges. Three separate messages to retire failed to reach 1st Bn. The Cheshire Regt. Result 800 casualties (Vol. I, pp. 104 and 105).
>
> Aug. 26th, Le Cateau. 2nd Bn. K.O.Y.L.I. and 1st Bn. Gordons failed to get the order to retire. Both battalions were decimated. (Vol. I, pp. 166 and 187.)
>
> Aug. 27th, Etreux. 2nd Bn. Munster Fusiliers, failed to get the message to retire though sent by two routes. The battalion was destroyed. (Vol. I, pp. 208-212.)

In addition to the above specific instances there was constant difficulty during the retreat in keeping rearguards informed of the situation of the main body.

The subject is of special interest at a time when the possibilities of wireless are being explored. (*Vide* Lesson 13.)

Manuals.—F.S.R., Vol. II, Sec. 44 (3), is sound in its precept, but hardly helpful in the solution of the problem confronting commanders in an operation such as the retreat from Mons.

Training.—The difficulties of communication hardly arise in peace time training. Officers and messengers are not shot—roads are not blocked with troops, transport and refugees—men and horses are well fed and fresh—the location of everyone is well known and easily found.

Hence false lessons are apt to be imbibed.

Lesson 6. (*March discipline*)

" Good marching depends on good march discipline." (F.S.R., Vol. II, Sec. 112 (1).)

Narrative.—The march discipline during the retreat was not always all that it should have been. This was due to commanders on arrival in the theatre of war accepting a lower standard of smartness and discipline than would be tolerated in peace time. By the time that the hardships of the retreat were encountered the leaders had lost control and were unable to regain it.

That this state of affairs was quite unnecessary was amply proved by many units who from the beginning maintained their peace time standard and were well repaid when the pinch came.

Note.—The above is not recorded in the official history and is from experience.

Manuals.—It is suggested that more stress might be laid in F.S.R., Vol. II, Sec. 112, on the real reason for the rules of march discipline.

It should be brought out somewhere that even second-rate troops can cut a fine figure when conditions are pleasant and easy, but it is when things are almost unendurable that the test really comes and the first rate troops emerge.

Training.—Our standard is high, but so it was in peace in 1914.

Other lessons from the period under review

Lesson 7. (Commander's orders must make his intention clear)

" Plans must be based on a logical and systematic analysis of the situation. The commander's orders must make his intention and the requirements of the situation clear to his subordinates." (F.S.R., Vol. II, Secs. 129. 7, 134. 1, 134. 4.)

Narrative.—G.H.Q. dispositions and orders during the operations leading up to the Battle of the Aisne seem hardly to have fulfilled these requirements. The orders issued for operations on Sept. 10th to 14th are all couched in the same terms (" The pursuit will be continued ") although the situation on each day was different and required specific handling.

Orders to the cavalry were vague, and there seems to have been no intimation to subordinate commanders that the gap between the German First and Second armies existed (Vol. I, p. 287), that German reinforcements from Maubeuge might be expected up to fill this gap, and that it was all important to forestall them on the Aisne.

Subordinate commanders, and certainly units, seem therefore to have been entirely innocent of any conception of the requirements of the situation. The outcome was that on Sept. 12th we failed to make a great effort to secure the crossings over the Aisne—on Sept. 13th the importance of time was overlooked (notably in the 2nd Division (Vol. I, pp. 328 and 332)), the cavalry were unaccountably inactive, and the Germans forestalled us on the Chemins-des-Dames. On Sept. 14th the B.E.F. blundered into a decisive battle without plan, control or co-ordination—(Vol. I, p. 341). A perusal of the story of events leading up to the Battle of the Aisne leads to the conclusion that clearer instructions and a more effective control by G.H.Q. might have altered in our favour the turn of events in the Aisne operations.

Manuals.—The sections of F.S.R., Vol. II, quoted above are clear and adequate.

Training.—Our exercises rarely deal with so complex a problem as confronted the C.-in-C. of the B.E.F.

Lesson 8.   (Factors affecting retention of ground unfavourable to defence)

" Excessive losses should not be incurred in order to hold ground which, though it has been gained, is subsequently found unsuitable." (F.S.R., Vol. II, Sec. 64. 14.)

Our policy on the Western front was never to give up an inch of ground unless forced by the enemy to do so, and in this latter contingency we often counter-attacked to recover ground of no tactical value. Hence our defensive line seldom lay on ground of our own choosing but was placed haphazard in any location where the Germans had held up our last offensive. These positions were therefore often sited on ground unsuitable for defence, devoid of observation, commanded by the enemy, waterlogged, insanitary, and difficult to place in a state of defence. The Ypres salient and Lys valley are well known examples (Vol. III, pp. 28, 69, 174).

The idea governing this policy seems to have been the preservation of our prestige among neutrals and the safeguarding of the morale of our own troops (Vol. III, p. 271).

The first reason seems hardly adequate. The Germans faced this risk without ill result in their retirement in 1917.—The fear of lowering the morale of the British soldier is quite absurd as proved in 1914 and 1918—his fighting value would have been increased rather than diminished by a withdrawal out of boggy regions to a dry and secure habitation.

It is suggested, therefore, that from a defensive point of view it would have been sounder (where sufficient depth in front of vital localities existed, *viz.*, Channel Ports) to have selected and strengthened the best possible defensive position in rear, and to have gone back to it when ready. It must, however, be remembered that the policy of the allies on the Western front was ultra offensive. Any withdrawal from close contact with the enemy would have increased the difficulty of resuming offensive action. The solution might, therefore, be to maintain outposts on the original forward position but to have the main defensive position some miles further back. This policy was adopted with great success in the Third Army about June 1918.

Manuals.—The quotation given above from F.S.R., Vol. II, Sec. 64 (14), states a principle quite clearly but seems to narrow the issue down too much to the avoidance of " Excessive Losses "—It is suggested that if the ground is unsuitable tactically (and strategically) it should be vacated.

Training.—The situation discussed above is rarely, if ever, introduced at peace exercises.

Lesson 9. (*Reinforcing success*)

Reinforcing success and not failure.

This precept is so well known that it is only mentioned so as to place on record an important lesson of the war.

Lesson 10. (*Factors affecting the issue of orders during a battle*)

" Orders must be issued to recipients in sufficient time to enable them to carry out the operation ordered at the appointed time." (F.S.R., Vol. II, Sec. 129. 3.)

" In case of partial success a commander must be guided in his decision as to future action by a consideration of the situation from every angle including the condition of his own troops." (F.S.R., Vol. II, Sec. 64. 13.)

Narrative.—These precepts were violated with unfortunate results on innumerable occasions. Notably at:—

    (*a*) *Aubers Ridge.*—After the failure with heavy loss of the initial attack of the 1st Division, the army commander ordered it to be renewed at 12 noon, then postponed it to 2.40 p.m., and then to 4 p.m. These orders and counter orders were issued without due appreciation either of the time it takes for orders to percolate through to the fighting troops, or to the condition of the troops who had incurred devastating losses on the morning attack (Vol. IV, pp. 23, 25). The result was that some units did not even reach the starting line until the attack of others had failed (Vol. IV, pp. 26 and 27).

        In the Meerut Division likewise orders showing a complete misconception of front line conditions led to great losses with no compensating success. (Vol. IV, p. 28.)

    (*b*) *Festubert.*—On the 18th May, 1915, the First Army Commander at 1.55 p.m. ordered the I Corps to launch an attack on La Quinque Rue at 4.30 p.m. The artillery bombardment was to commence at 2.30 p.m.

        The main attack (by I Corps order) was to be carried out by the 3rd Canadian Brigade (right), and the 4th Guards Brigade (left).

        Owing to the late transmission of orders the artillery bombardment did not commence until 3 p.m., and the 3rd Canadian Brigade did not arrive on the battlefield until 5.20 p.m., by which time the Guards had been repulsed. (Vol. IV, pp. 71, 72, 73.)

(c) *Loos.*—On the 25th September the initial attack of the 28th Infantry Brigade (9th Division) failed with enormous loss.

The Brigadier endeavoured to reinforce his leading troops with his Brigade reserve and incurred further loss and achieved nothing. At 11.15 a.m. the corps commander, labouring under a misconception of the situation, ordered a renewal of the attack by the 28th Brigade at 12.15 p.m. In spite of the confusion and losses resulting from the two previous attacks against uncut wire, the 28th Brigade managed to launch one and a half battalions again at 12.15 p.m. (A notable achievement.)

The attack of course failed with loss. The 28th Brigade was for the moment incapable of further offensive action (Vol. IV, pp. 242 and 243).

These instances can be multiplied.

It is important to remember that lack of information from the front was the reason why higher commanders so often entirely failed to gauge the true state of affairs, and this in turn was mainly due to lack of communications. (*Vide* Lessons 12 and 13.)

Manuals.—The above quoted paras. of F.S.R., Vol. II, cover these lessons.

Training.—It is generally understood that orders must be issued in good time. It is perhaps not so clearly appreciated that this is only possible if orders are short. The complication of modern war has led not only to an increase in the length of operation orders, but also to the issue of innumerable lengthy operation instructions, notably to the Royal Air Force. It must take a considerable time to prepare and reproduce all this literature; hence operations will have to be delayed in order to enable the orders to get out, and we may lose the battle while we are writing orders.

The solution would seem to be to train our army and air force to act on the briefest orders, and to discourage the staff from issuing super-perfect orders in peace, which would be impossible in war.

Again it is doubtful if the material and moral condition of troops who have carried out an attack is considered sufficiently during training.

During the war commanders seemed to be influenced by field day conditions, and to fail to realize that a unit that has been heavily engaged is no longer the perfect and easily controlled machine it was before it set out on its venture. This seems the key to many of the injudicious orders issued.

Lesson 11. (*Long drawn out battles and the difficulties of a commander*)

" For political or strategic reasons a commander is often required to fight under conditions unfavourable to the success of his own Force."

Narrative.—The Battle of Loos was undertaken against the judgment of the British leaders (Vol. IV, p. 129). By the evening of the first day of the battle (Sept. 25th) the advantage of the initial tactical surprise had passed, a fleeting opportunity of success had been missed, and a successful outcome to the battle was unlikely. (Vol. IV, p. 267.)

On this day our casualties totalled some 470 officers and 15,000 other ranks.

The battle was, however, continued until early in November, achieved nothing, and cost us, in the First Army alone, a total of 2,013 officers and 48,367 other ranks. (Vol. IV, p. 391.)

It is often asked why our leaders persevered in so costly a battle offering so little prospect of an adequate return.

The reasons which forced them to continue the battle were the same as those which compelled them to launch it. Our French allies were carrying out a major offensive on our right and were insistent on our co-operation. In view of the unfavourable situation on the Russian front Lord Kitchener considered an offensive in the West essential. He, therefore, directed the British C.-in-C. to do his utmost to help the French offensive although this might entail heavy loss. (Vol. IV, p. 129.) The continuance of the Entente might depend on the effectiveness of the co-operation of the British in the French offensive plans (Vol. IV, p. 395). In view of these instructions the British leaders were constrained to continue the battle so long as the French were in need of our co-operation. (Vol. IV, p. 267 and p. 391.)

The conditions under which the battle of Loos was fought make one realize the complexity of the issues governing a commander's decision in war, and the burden of responsibility which he carries.

Such were the reasons for the continuance of the Loos offensive. It must be admitted, however, that our excessive casualties were often due to bad staff work, to the issue of orders impossible of execution, and to a multiplication of the errors referred to in Lesson 10.

Lesson 12. (*Information*)

The conduct of a battle depends largely on early and accurate information.

Narrative.—This statement is fully borne out by the lessons of the War. Without information a commander is powerless to influence the battle with his reserves. At Loos and other battles many of the injudicious decisions given by commanders were due to lack of information, inaccurate information, or failure to sift its reliability. (*Vide* Lessons 10 and 15.)

Manuals.—The manuals are sound but perhaps more stress should be laid in F.S.R., Vol. II, on commanders sending forward to get information and not being content to await it from the fighting troops who may be dead, or have other pre-occupations.

The importance of information as to the condition of our own troops should be brought out.

Training.—Peace battles move so quickly, and projectiles being absent, it is difficult to introduce the war problem of information.

Perhaps the troops might be induced to be a little more inquisitive and informative, but above all commanders should have personnel definitely earmarked to go forward and get information.

Lesson 13. (*Communications*)

The provision of information, and the rapid distribution of orders is dependent on communications.

Narrative.—The extent to which the value of communications was realized in the war is reflected in the labour and energy displayed in their provision.

The many regrettable incidents during the retreat from Mons, due to lack of communications, have been indicated in Lesson 5. As already shown in Lesson 10, many of the disastrous decisions given by commanders on the Western front were due to lack of information as a result of absence of communications. To the same cause may be traced the constant late arrival of orders.

Lateral communication during all stages (mobile and static) of the war was a matter of extreme difficulty.

The vital necessity of communications can hardly be in doubt. The main difficulty is communication with the business end of the battle—*i.e.*, with the units actually fighting. Cable, never reliable in the forward area, becomes less so now owing to the havoc caused to wires by mechanical vehicles. Liaison officers in the forward area are not dependable, as proved in 1914 and from experience in trench warfare. They have to walk and are consequently too slow—they cannot get their information back—they get hit, lost, and never arrive. They are a useful adjunct, but as the prior means of communication, are quite inadequate, except on field days.

Wireless at the headquarters of each fighting unit seems, therefore, the only solution. (*Vide* Lesson 5.)

Manuals.—F.S.R., Vol. II, Chap. XIII, is wholehearted in its precepts on communications.

In other portions of the manual the subject is dealt with perhaps a little nebulously, and hardly makes its importance stand out until we come to static warfare (Sec. 74. 10) where some enthusiasm on the subject is displayed.

Training.—The subject is always considered. It is doubtful, however, if full weight is given to it. Do signal officers attend all formation exercises with their commanders?

Are they required to play their part in the conduct of operations?

Lesson 14. *(Defence, Surprise)*

Surprise is as important in defence as in attack.

Narrative.—In the Boer war the power of small arm fire in defence was clearly demonstrated. This lesson was expensively confirmed in the late war.

In South Africa we had a vast superiority in artillery—yet at Colenso and in the other battles of 1899, our guns were entirely ineffective against the concealed Boer marksmen. In the late war the concealed machine gun dominated the battle-field. It is to be noted, however, that in both wars the defensive power of small arm fire depended on concealment—once the defenders' small arm weapons are located their sting has been drawn, and the balance of advantage reverts to the attack with its possession of the initiative and power of manœuvre.

Manuals and training.—Whilst the defensive power of small arm fire is well recognized, it is doubtful if there is a full realization that this power depends almost entirely on concealment and surprise.

The ideal should be for the enemy to be kept completely in the dark as to the defenders' location and dispositions—he should never be able to divine what he is up against, which is the main position and which merely screen, on what targets to concentrate his artillery or where to put in his attack. Those present at the battle of Colenso do not yet know what positions were held by the Boers!

The above entails concealment, which it must be admitted is not easy in the hasty occupation of a position, and this difficulty gives hope to the attack in mobile warfare.

It is questionable whether the defensive dispositions habitual during training fulfil the requirements of concealment and surprise. It would rarely require a magician on the attacking side to size up exactly where " the line of foremost defended localities " lies—we know little about camouflage—machine guns are difficult to conceal. It is suggested that the rather obvious dispositions taken up my our infantry in defence are due to an exaggerated desire for artillery observation (F.S.R., Vol. II, Sec. 78 (4) and (6))—which is apt to force the infantry forward into exposed positions. Perhaps more could be done in balancing the conflicting requirements of concealment and observation, and due weight given to the consideration that in defence it is small arms fire (and not artillery) which is going to stop the enemy (I.T., Vol. II, Sec. 21. 6 (1926) and I.T., Vol. II, Sec. 21. 11 (1931)) unless it has been neutralized by hostile artillery and machine guns; this latter contingency will occur if our defences are located.

If concealment and surprise are essential in defence (F.S.R., Vol. II, Sec. 78. 3) it would seem desirable (or indeed essential) to· have protective troops in front of the main position so as to keep the enemy guessing, induce him to make his fire plan under false premises, and render his artillery as inaffective as ours in South Africa.

This question is controversial and is only mentioned here to bring it to notice. It will suffice to indicate that F.S.R., Vol. II, in its attack chapter clearly contemplates our potential enemies having protective troops and outposts in front of their defensive positions. (Sec. 60. 3 and 62. 1.) In the chapter on defence F.S.R. weakens and has it both ways (Sec. 78. 8, 80. 3, 80. 5).

These paragraphs have puzzled many. In practice defensive fire plans and arrangements are apt to ignore the question.

The vital point to realize is that once small arm weapons are located they need no longer inspire terror.

Lesson 15. (*Difficulty in the conduct of a battle after the initial phase*)

The plan for battle must include arrangements not only for capturing the enemy's foremost defences, but also for ensuring a continuous and sustained effort throughout every stage of the battle with a view to giving the enemy neither time nor respite to bring up his reserves.

Narrative.—The battle of Loos is an example of a successful " break-in " failing to materialize into a " break-through ", and of an auspicious beginning ending in failure with some 50,000 casualties. The reasons for this unhappy ending are worth exploring.

This battle was fought, for strategic reasons and with a view to assisting our French allies, against the advice of our commanders, with insufficient numbers, equipment and ammunitions, and at a time and place not of their choosing. (Vol. IV, p. 129.) Despite this unfavourable setting the battle only missed being successful by a narrow margin of time. The question of interest is whether more skilful conduct of the battle would have placed this time margin in our favour.

The story of the battle is briefly as follows:—

After a four days' bombardment the attack was launched under cover of gas at 6.30 a.m. on 25th Sept. with six divisions —from right to left 47th, 15th, 1st, 9th, 2nd—The rôles of the flank divisions were to form defensive flanks. The other four divisions were given almost unlimited objectives and stress was laid on pushing on with the utmost rapidity. (Vol. IV, App. 16, 17, 21.)

All divisions, except the (2nd) were successful in breaking through the enemy's first position, but the right brigade of the 1st Division was held up for several hours and the left brigade of the 9th Division was unable to advance.

The remainder pressed forward and for a time there seemed a prospect of their reaching the strongly wired German second position before it was manned. (*Vide* German anxiety, Vol. IV, p. 304.)

We were, however, unable to follow up our initial success, the Germans were given time to bring up their reserves, and we were eventually confronted by these reserves occupying their second position behind wire fifteen yards wide. (*Vide* Vol. IV, p. 120.)

Our chance had gone (Vol. IV, pp. 221, 234, 244, 247).

The main reasons for our failure to exploit a fleeting opportunity seem to have been:—

(*a*) Lack of control of leading battalions and failure to reorganize and get balanced after each bound.

The two leading brigades of the 15th Division, after capturing the Loos defences, pushed on without reorganizing, with the result that they lost direction, went South instead of West, and upset the whole divisional plan—an expensive lesson in the importance of reorganizing. (Vol. IV, pp. 202, 203.)

(*b*) Brigade reserves were piled upon leading battalions and accordingly became involved in their disorganization.

(*c*) Divisional reserves were not employed with a specific offensive rôle of their own. It is true that in the 7th and 9th Divisions they were given such rôles during the battle, but seem to have been imbued with the idea of reinforcing, never got going, and finally simply got involved in the hold up of the leading brigades.

(*d*) Army reserves were so far back that they could not intervene on the first day.

(*e*) Finally lack of information, and too ready acceptance of available reports, led to very unfortunate decisions, notably as to the employment of the 21st and 24th Divisions (Vol. IV, pp. 282, 283). (*Vide* Lesson 13.)

B

It would be fruitless to speculate as to how the battle would have developed if conducted differently.

The lesson, however, stands out clearly in this battle (as at Festubert, Cambrai, and The Somme) that the conduct of a battle after the initial stage is far more difficult than the staging of the opening attack.

Those conditions will obtain even more fully in mobile warfare owing to the situation being more fluid and the enemy's position less assured.

Hence we must study the problem of how to achieve a ' break-through ''—As the whole problem is bound up with circumventing the small arms fire of the defence, it may be well to consider the different phases of the attack battle in that light. (*Vide* Lesson 14.)

Lesson 16. (Attack. How to discount defensive S.A. fire. Contact. Break-in. Break-through. Surprise. Manœuvre.)

(*a*) On the Western front the concealed machine gun, plus thick wire obstacles and no flanks, dominated the battlefield and gave a marked superiority to the defence. How in the future can this defensive power of small arm fire be neutralized in attack?

(*b*) In the late war the problem was first dealt with by the provision of masses of heavy artillery and the expenditure of an unlimited amount of ammunition, with a view to blotting out the whole of the enemy's defensive system, and of destroying his unlocated machine guns in the general havoc.

This crude method rendered surprise impossible and often failed in its first purpose of neutralizing the enemy's machine guns (Aubers Ridge and The Somme). Later the introduction of tanks restored the power of surprise with consequent success.

(*c*) The next war which we are contemplating will probably be in the nature of a major expedition—our potential enemy will probably not be in possession of great resources in all the modern adjuncts to war. He will have flanks, and the problem of heavy wire entanglements will be absent, at any rate in the early stages. No matter, however, who our enemy may be, he is certain to be well provided with small arm weapons.

How are we going to deal with them? The lavish provision of heavy guns and colossal expenditure of ammunition, as in the late war, will be out of the question.

During training we are apt to pin our faith on every occasion on a comprehensive fire plan which takes some hours to mount.

(*d*) *Contact.*—The situation on gaining contact with the enemy will first be considered. When the leading troops of advanced guards are held up by such a display of enemy small arms fire that the commander has to take some action, it is suggested that the comprehensive fire plan solution, culminating in an attack on the direct route of advance, is not always a satisfactory decision. The situation at this period will be fluid and the opposing troops mobile. The long inactive pause during the preparation of the fire plan will leave the enemy free to manœuvre as he pleases, and by the time the fire plan is ready the situation may have completely altered.

What then is the answer? Our operations on Le Petit Morin in 1914 may give us a clue.

In those days we were not very clever at fire plans, but we had the power of manœuvre—The I and II Corps managed with small loss to manœuvre the enemy out of his positions. (Vol. I, pp. 283, 284, 285.) It is true that these operations took from five to eight hours, but this time could be shortened with our present-day knowledge of the combined action of all arms. It is to be noted, however, that on the III Corps front, where the enemy intended a protracted resistance, we made little headway in the absence of a comprehensive fire plan.

Although the manœuvre operations of the I and II Corps were nearly as slow as our fire plan habits, they were effective, kept the enemy engaged on his whole front, discovered where the Germans were strong and where weak, and obviated attacking him where strongest.

If the desirability of manœuvre on a wide front during contact operations is agreed to, it follows that this operation can be carried out best by mobile troops. The corollary is that in suitable country tanks should be included in advanced guards. In any case prior to contact formations should advance on battle fronts, so as to engage the enemy all along his front, and not be caught in the dilemma of the 1st Division on the Aisne on the 14th Sept., 1914. (Vol. I, pp. 341-347.)

(e) *Main attack.*—We now turn to the problem of dealing with the hostile small arms fire where resistance is such as to entail a comprehensive plan. His machine guns will be unlocated—his position concealed—his intentions obscure.

The attackers' problem is:—

(a) To break-in.
(b) To break-through.

(f) *Break-in.*—To effect the initial " break-in " he must of course have a comprehensive fire plan and has to decide between concentration of fire on likely machine gun posts, or on a creeping barrage. The first is rather a gamble and may be ineffective—the second can deal with a strictly limited frontage owing to lack of guns and ammunition. Neither in itself is entirely convincing.

He may employ tanks for the " break-in " operations, but he will require these for the subsequent " break-through " as will be shown later.

It seems, therefore, that he must enlist the advantages of indirect attack where possible, concealment, and surprise, if he is to make sure of circumventing the enemy small arm fire.

On the Western front, owing to the absence of flanks the indirect method of attack is not to be found. As already stated there will probably be exposed flanks in a major expedition and opportunities for this manœuvre.

Concealment and surprise were difficult to achieve in France, but where they were employed the results were astonishing. Good examples are the Third Army operations at Cambrai, Nov., 1937, the Fourth Army attack on the 8th Aug., 1918, the German attack under cover of fog in 1918, the Third Army night attack at Ayette, 2nd April, 1918—Towards the end of the war nearly all our attacks were launched in the half light before dawn.

The conclusion, therefore, would seem to be that in addition to fire plans and mechanical support, success in the initial stage of an attack, in the future as in the past, will depend on concealment (night, fog, smoke, ground) manœuvre and surprise.

(g) *Break-through* (*Vide* Lesson 15).—Once the crust has been broken the problem is to maintain the momentum of the attack so as to capture the whole enemy defensive system before he has time to gauge the situation or bring up his reserves— time is now all important—a margin of an hour or so will decide which side snatches the victory (Loos, Lesson 15).

This stage is no pursuit, but hard fighting. It is futile to order the troops expended in the initial assault to carry on the " break-through " as at Loos. Fresh reserves immediately available where success has been achieved are essential.

Infantry move too slowly for this purpose; cavalry has not the necessary offensive power.

This therefore seems to be the opportunity for tanks, supported by infantry as soon as the latter can be got up. Failing tanks a definite force of all arms, made as mobile as possible, should be earmarked and manœuvred for this purpose.

(h) *Pursuit.*—After the break-through and not before, as seems often to have been expected in France, the pursuit stage opens.

Whether the above conclusions are sound or otherwise, the one thing that is certain is that there can be no stereotyped way of fighting a battle and we must avoid a too hidebound mentality on the subject. Manœuvre and surprise are the key to the problem.

Manuals.—F.S.R., Sec. 62. 4, seems to contain an invitation to attack the enemy where he is strongest. In Sec. 64, the " break-through " phase does not stand out very clearly, while Sec. 75 is hardly adequate. Many seem to confuse this phase with " pursuit " (a relic of war conceptions).

F.S.R., Vol. II, is not very forcible in its injunctions as to the conduct of a battle, *i.e.*, Sec. 61 (2) seems to advocate both a limited and unlimited objective, while Sec. 64 (8) and (9) suggest unlimited objectives. Sec. 64. 7 advocates keeping touch but also losing it. The spirit of these dictums is clear enough but the wording perhaps unconvincing.

Training.—Perhaps we concentrate during training too much on the opening stage of an attack at the expense of the later and more difficult stages.

The time it takes to prepare a comprehensive fire plan is now well understood. It is now for our fire producers to tell us what sort of support they can provide in a much shorter time.

Fire plans must be used tactically in conjunction with surprise and manoeuvre—The enemy must not be forgotten during their preparation. We must try to avoid being too inelastic.

Lesson 17. (*Mobility. Preservation of energy*)

(*a*) In previous lessons stress has been laid on the importance of manoeuvre and surprise. These requirements imply stamina, morale, and consequently the preservation of energy.

(*b*) A study of the war from the first day at Mons to the last day of the advance in 1918 leaves one impressed with the continuous physical and mental strain imposed on the infantry soldier. He must be ever capable of manoeuvre over any sort of country under fire—on reaching his objective he must be in a physical condition to defend, and to prepare for defence, his new position, and be in a mental condition to withstand the uncertainties, alarms and horrors of war.

It is doubtful if the supreme importance of the conservation of energy as a battle winning requirement was realized in the war.

(*c*) In order to enable the infantry soldier to be in a fit state to withstand the great calls on his endurance there are three essentials.

(i) He must be well fed. In this we seldom failed him, except in the notorious case of the 21st and 24th Divisions at Loos. (Vol. IV, pp. 277, 279, 285, 318.)

(ii) He must embark on his perilous adventure fresh and " full of beans ".

This requirement was not always fulfilled. (Loos, Vol. IV, pp. 159-161; Somme, Vol. V, pp. 286, 305, 313.) In most of our trench warfare battles it was overlooked that if the infantry marched all night to form up, and fought all day, their stamina was exhausted by the following evening. Hence probably many of our retirements in 1917 about dusk from positions previously captured.

(iii) The soldier's load must be reduced to a minimum.

In 1914 we went to Mons wearing packs, great coats, etc. These we discarded on the retreat.

During this battle we were issued with an extra bandolier of ammunition, and were saddled with it for the retreat to the great detriment of stamina.

From 1915 onwards the soldier entered a battle carrying every conceivable article of offence and defence. It is understood that he also favoured carrying all his souvenirs irrespective of weight, but soon shed most of the other impedimenta. This impossible and cumbrous load hampered his movements and undermined his stamina.

It is impossible to quote specific instances, but there can be little doubt that many cases of want of elan and tenacity were due to exhaustion.

In short, preservation of energy was not given due weight. Our " Man management " was on a far lower level than our " Horse management ".

Manuals.—There is nothing in the manuals prescribing the husbanding of life and energy.

Training.—There are few indications on manœuvres that much attention is paid to the conservation of energy. It is understood that methods of lightening the weight carried by the infantry soldier are under consideration. In this connection two points may be of value :—

(i) No instance has been found recorded of the infantry running short of S.A.A. This is, however, not conclusive as he often carried two extra bandoliers.

(ii) The introduction of automatic weapons adds to the weight carried by the infantryman and tends to immobilize him. While rejoicing over a lighter automatic weapon we must not forget that the ammunition load remains the same.

Lesson 18. (*Minor operations—Raids*)

Closely bound up with the question of the preservation of life and energy is the one of the advisability of minor offensives in the intervals between major operations.

(*a*) The policy of the British Army in this respect was laid down by G.H.Q in March, 1915. Local offensives were to be carried out constantly with a view to :—

(i) Improving the morale of our troops.
(ii) Lowering that of the enemy.
(iii) Securing identifications.
(iv) Misleading the enemy as to the location of impending offensives (Vol. III, p. 33).

(*b*) This policy was faithfully adhered to throughout the war. While our French allies, with the apparent connivance of our enemies, maintained a sort of unofficial suspension of arms on their quiet fronts (Vol. V, p. 156) our arrival in a hitherto peaceful area at once heralded a veritable tornado of offensiveness, quite regardless of our relative advantages with the enemy as to ground, armaments and position (Vimy Ridge, Vol. V, p. 212), Nieuport, June, 1917. Our aggressive spirit was displayed by Raids, Sniping, and Fire surprises. The success of these measures in attaining the intended results is considered below.

(*c*). *Raids*.—If the primary object of raids was to improve the morale of our troops it may be at once admitted that, as conducted, they completely failed in their purpose. They were generally carried out with no definite object but to be frightful. They were often staged under conditions entirely detrimental to their success. (Vol. V, p. 156.) The best leaders and the best men were necessarily selected for these operations, and irreplaceable material was thus expended for quite nebulous reasons, our casualties were great, everyone hated them, and their delivery for insufficient reason has left a bitterness among the fighting troops which is reflected in war literature and stage productions. As a morale raiser they may be definitely ruled out (at any rate as conducted on the Western front).

There can, however, be no doubt that they must have been wearying to the enemy. While this is true, they were probably far more costly to ourselves in life and energy.

In their third purpose of securing identifications there were occasions when they served their purpose and were fully justified. (Somme, Vol. V, pp. 306-307.)

As regards their final object of deceiving the enemy as to the location of future offensives, they seem to have achieved a measure of success on the Somme (Vol. V, p. 310), but at Vivy Ridge, In May, 1916, do not appear to have achieved advantages commensurate with the hardships and casualties imposed on the troops. (Vol. V, p. 213.)

From the above the conclusion would seem to be that minor offensives are justifiable only as a definite military operation for a specific purpose conducing to the success of the commander's plan. They have no place in the conduct of war when carried out merely as a sort of competition between formations with no specific military object, and when needlessly ordered they impair the confidence of the troops in their leaders and lower their morale.

Sniping.—Judging by our own experience of the German snipers this habit is distinctly disconcerting to the opposing side. It is especially valuable in making reconnaissance difficult.

Fire surprises.—The efficacy of this method of maintaining the offensive spirit rather depends on which side is most surprised. We had a habit of forgetting this truism. At Nieuport in June, 1917, being vastly inferior to the Germans in artillery, we proceeded to give him some " fire surprises "— he acknowledged his surprise by blowing us almost off the ground with his superior armament.

It would seem that only with considerable superiority in fire power should fire surprises be initiated.

General.—A further factor in the problem of whether to keep the front quiet or otherwise, is that continual fighting militates against the improvement of defences.

Hence in deciding on a policy in this respect, due weight must be given as to whether plans for the future are offensive or defensive. (Vimy, Vol. V, p. 213.)

Lesson 19. (*Counter-attacks. Variation of method. Surprise*)

The essence of a successful counter-attack lies in surprise.

(I) In considering this subject it is well to clear one's mind as to the object of a counter attack. This object is:—

(*a*) To recover ground vital to the operations on hand.

(*b*) To exploit an opportunity of " scuppering " the enemy with little loss to oneself. The Boers were adepts at this class of operation.

(II) On the Western front nearly all our counter-attacks were delivered for the recovery of ground which had little tactical value. For instance at the first battle of Ypres on the 23rd October, 1914, the Korteker Cabaret was counter-attacked and recovered with great loss, but had then to be abandoned as untenable. (Vol. II, p. 187.)

We were slowly learning this lesson towards the end of the war.

(III) A study of the multitude of counter-attacks delivered in the war leads to the conclusion that the essential factor for success is surprise.

This surprise may be achieved by a variety of ways according to the situation, enemy value and methods, ground, etc., on one occasion the opportunity for surprise may lie in immediate execution, in another in skilful use of ground, in another in very deliberate preparation.

In the first battle of Ypres the majority of our counter-attacks, although by no means methodically prepared, were successful. The reason seems to have been that in this battle the German leading units had unlimited objectives, were untrained in consolidating each objective as gained, and through no wile of ours were nearly always surprised. (Vol. II, p. 199.)

In the second battle of Ypres we pursued the same methods but were nearly always unsuccessful. A reason in addition to that of faulty organization was that the Germans had been drilled to our methods, learnt their lesson, and advanced by limited objectives, making each good in turn. No longer were they surprised by our poorly organized counter-attacks, and failing the element of surprise we failed dismally with heavy loss. In the trench warfare period we again find surprise counter-attacks succeeding (German attacks, Loos, Quarries and Boes Hugo, Vol. IV, pp. 302 and 320) while those lacking the element of surprise failed.

The attempts of Cartiers Fora, which lacked every essential for success, to recapture the Quarries on 26th Sept. failed (Vol. IV, p. 345)—on the other hand a well organized deliberate counter-attack to recapture Chalk Pit Copse on 27th Sept. succeeded—in this case surprise was achieved by weight of shells and perfection of organization (Vol. IV, p. 360).

(IV) The lessons that seem to emerge from the above are:—

(a) A counter-attack must have a definite purpose and be conducted in accordance with common sense (e.g., The rules of war).
ducted on hard and fast lines.
on hard and fast lines.
Methods must be varied according to the situation, type and probable action of the enemy; methods suitable to a first Ypres may be suicidal at a second battle of that name.

(c) Whether a counter-attack be termed " Immediate " or " deliberate " no stereotyped rule can be laid down as to method, time required to organize, or fire power required to support.
To achieve surprise is the main essential and the facilities for its attainment are a guiding factor in deciding on the most judicious time for launching the counter-attack.

Manuals.—It is suggested that F.S.R., Vol. II, Sec. 82, conveys the impression that there is no counter-attack feasible between one delivered immediately the enemy has captured an objective, and one delivered after a great lapse of time with all the paraphernalia of fire plan, etc. Where, as will often be the case, it is neither possible nor desirable, to hurl troops at the enemy immediately he arrives, the provision of surprise may attain the object a few hours later. F.S.R. does not seem to contemplate surprise, except in the case where it is feasible to attack instantly. Infantry Training, Sec. 26 (5), is more elastic in its conception of the subject, and does mention surprise in Sec. 26. 7.

In this manual as in F.S.R. the balance between fire plan and surprise perhaps favours the former too greatly.

Neither manual is very explicit as to the object justifying a counter-attack.

Training.—This is in accordance with the manuals.

Lesson 20. (*Entrenchments or wire*)

The lesson of the dominating influence in the late war on operations and equipment of entrenchments and wire, in conjunction with hidden small arm weapons, needs no elaboration.

From the moment the first shot was fired at Mons everyone tried to get the protection of a trench.

Manuals.—There is little in the manuals to indicate the importance of the subject.

F.S.R., Vol. II, Sec. 14, treats the subject under the heading " Engineers " while in Sec. 10 (Infantry) no reference is made to the subject. In I.T., Vol. II, Sec. 8, the subject is again dealt with under an Engineer heading; in Chapter 8 the detail of working parties is adequately dealt with.

Perhaps a more robust lead is required to stimulate a belief in entrenchments as an important cog in the machinery of war.

Training.—For obvious reasons the technical and tactical employment of field defences is a difficult subject to deal with during peace training.

Training in field defences is being developed and no doubt some interest aroused in the subject (Army Training Memo. No. 6, Para. 8).

Our training curriculum includes no consideration of static, or semi-static, warfare either as attackers or defenders. It is for consideration whether a complete disregard of the subject is wise. Sooner or later, in any campaign, we are certain to have to face the problem in some shape.

Lesson 21. (*Selection and training of commanders*)

A study of the operations on the Western front leaves one impressed both with the far reaching influence of the method in which command is exercised, and with the extraordinary difficulties under which a commander labours. The pressure of allies, politics, events on other fronts, etc., constantly forces him to undertake operations of which he entirely disapproves (Mons, Vol. I, p. 261. Loos, Vol. IV, p. 393. Somme, Vol. V, p. 51).

In view of the difficulties of their task of its vital importance, perhaps the most outstanding lesson of the war is the necessity for the utmost care in the selection of Commanders in war, and the importance of training them during peace for their rôle.

The question of training will be referred to again in Part V.

PART III.—ORGANIZATION AND EQUIPMENT

Lesson 1. (Wireless)

The importance of developing wireless in order to strengthen the machinery of command has already been dealt with in lesson 13.

Lesson 2. (Covering fire weapons)

Artillery and tanks in attack are the natural enemies of the hidden defensive machine gun. Automatic small arms weapons have increased in numbers enormously since the war. Our artillery gun power is, however, about the same as in 1914, and our Tank power small. Our offensive power does not, therefore, seem to have increased in the same ratio as that of defensive weapons.

Lesson 3. (Proportion of 18 prs. and Hows.)

Our experiences in the early part of the war, notably on the Aisne, point to the advisability of increasing the number of howitzers in our divisional artilleries at the expense of fewer 18 prs. It is realized that this question has been considered and it is only mentioned here as a record.

PART IV.—ADMINISTRATION

Our administrative arrangements on the Western front were admirable.

Perhaps the most striking administrative lesson of the war was the expansion of our forces and resources after the outbreak of war (Vol. II, pp. 2-19, Vol. V, Chap. IV, Vol. VI)— a stupendous task in view of our absence of peace preparation (Vide Part I of this report).

Part V.—Training (General)

The following remarks on training are in elaboration, or in addition, to those contained in Part II at the end of each lesson.

1. *General.*—One of the most marked re-actions from the war has been the great advance in our methods of training, and the extraordinary interest taken in the subject throughout the army. The army is probably more highly trained than ever before.

In taking stock, however, in the light of war lessons, there are certain points worthy of consideration.

2. *Scope of our training.*—(a) It is questionable whether our training is not too narrow in its scope, and too rigid in its conception.

We concentrate on " mobile warfare "—in our interpretation of this sort of warfare neither side pauses for any appreciable time, nor are wire, strong entrenchments, or similar inconveniences encountered.

Our attack exercises are apt to deal exclusively with the problem of breaking through the crust of the enemy's defences. Solutions to this problem are rapidly becoming almost standardized. The tendency is for a fire plan, without either surprise or manœuvre, to be accepted as the panacea for all ills, while scant attention is paid to the enemy's character, armament or probable action.

(b) Nearly all the battles of the war, in either mobile or trench warfare, from the German's experiences at the 1st Ypres to our own throughout the war up to 1918, proved that the most difficult nut to crack was to effect a " breakthrough " after a " break-in ". Yet we give this phase of the battle little attention during training.

F.S.R., Vol. II, is much below its usual standard when dealing with this subject, Sec. 75, while being inadequate, hardly paints the true picture.

The " break-through " phase of a battle seems to be a war lesson which we have missed. (*Vide* Lessons 15 and 16.)

(c) Even within the limited compass of our training exercises the problems set are too orderly, and the available information too complete, to give a war flavour to the exercise by the introduction of the uncertainties, fears and disappointments of war.

No vital decisions are needed to cope with most of our peace problems. It is usually obvious whether attack, defence, or retirement is the right answer—and all that remains is to decide how to do it.

War is more difficult than this—the prior and most difficult problem is " what to do " and the later one of " how to do it " has to be solved under more perplexing conditions than obtain at our rather orderly exercises.

(*d*) Officers get ample and sound guidance in official publications and conferences as to the tactical handling of troops. With so much advice available there is a danger of the officer seeking the answer to a specific problem from a page in a book rather than from common sense reinforced by well digested military knowledge. When he errs, he is apt to lament his folly in having got on to the wrong page rather than to blame his lack of judgment and common sense. (*Vide* para. 5 on Individuality.)

In short there is a danger of our getting too narrow in our conceptions and hide bound in our methods.

(*e*) Army Training Instructions No. 4A gives a broad lead as to how to counteract the tendencies noted above. The only addition which is suggested to this pamphlet is that a clear indication should be given that the uncertainties and " fog of war " should be introduced in tactical exercises, and the " break-through " phases of a battle studied.

It would not be surprising if this latter study had reactions on our methods of defence.

3. *Training of commanders.*—The vital importance during peace of training commanders for their rôle in war has been referred to in lesson 21.

It is difficult to suggest any improvement in our present methods beyond those contained in para. 2, but the following observations may tend towards keeping higher commanders in their proper sphere of considering the higher problems of war :—

(*a*) It should be an axiom that the object of a higher formation exercise is to practise the commanders serving immediately under the director in the command of their own, or of a higher formation. This object must be kept in view throughout the exercise, and time not wasted on minor tactics, which are the province of lesser people.

(*b*) In higher formation exercises divisional and higher commanders must not be allowed to see more of the ground and situation than would be possible in war.

(*c*) Manœuvres are of real value in testing the machinery of command. They further give the troops experience in competing with the discomforts of war.

(*d*) Finally it is suggested that Training and Manœuvre Regulations should deal separately with the training of higher commanders and that of regimental officers. The two problems are entirely different.

4. *Night operations*.—Much has been said in this paper about the necessity of surprise. Do we study the employment of night operations sufficiently?

In attack, apart from the well known difficulties of operating in the dark, the fixed lines of the defenders' machine guns are the greatest danger to be circumvented. The subject merits thought and trial.

5. *Individuality*.—Much stress in late years has been laid on the development of individuality in the soldier and some progress achieved in the lower ranks.

It is, however, doubtful if this progress applies to the officer, notably in the infantry.

Everything is now so highly organized and supervised from above that even energy in sports and games is apt to reflect more the idiosyncracies of the commander than the spirit of the unit. The character of a unit, a priceless quality in war, is apt to be undermined by too much inspiration from above as to work and play. The question is a delicate one but is important.

6. *Capacity to act quickly*.—The disastrous consequences of ill conceived and belated orders have been referred to in Part II, Lesson 10. There is, however, another side to the question. No matter how perfect our staff arrangements, the very character of war will produce sudden and unexpected situations requiring immediate action. In 1914 units were literally hurled into action without explanation or apology.

In these sudden and startling situations the orthodox programme of conferences, reconnaissances and detailed plans are out of the question. There must be a plan, but a quick one and immediate action.

Our peace exercises should include situations to accustom leaders to dealing with this contingency.

Perhaps we are getting slow.

7. *Training in theatre of war*.—(a) F.S.R., Vol. I, Sec. 5 (1), lays down the responsibility of a commander for the training of his troops in the theatre of war.

This responsibility entails his being provided with machinery to deal with the training of his troops.

An organization must therefore be in being for providing him with:—

(a) A training directorate;

(b) An organization and competent instructors for a strictly limited number of schools of instruction;

(c) A staff to study the training lessons of the war and to produce the necessary literature on the subject.

The scope of such an organization will depend on the location, class and development of the war, but a skeleton should be thought out in peace.

(b) The question has been raised as to whether manuals of the "potted precept type" should be prepared for the use of personnel raised during a war. On the whole it is suggested that this is unnecessary. A paragraph showing the distribution of staff duties might be added to F.S.R., Vol. I, but otherwise the existing manuals of each arm should suffice. A programme of training for specific periods for personnel raised during war should, however, exist.

CONCLUSION

8. In looking back at the war and all its lessons we must not overlook the most important lesson of them all, *viz.*: All wars produce new methods and fresh problems. The last war was full of surprises—the next one is likely to be no less prolific in unexpected developments—Hence we must study the past in the light of the probabilities of the future, which is what really matters. No matter, however, how prophetic we may be, the next war will probably take a shape far different to our peace-time conceptions. In order to cope with this upset to our preconceived ideas our leaders must be versatile, mentally robust, and full of common sense and self reliance. To produce this sort of mentality must be the object of our training.

(Signed) A. E. McNAMARA.
Major-General.

APPENDIX II

REPORT ON OPERATIONS ON THE WESTERN FRONT BY MAJOR-GENERAL J. KENNEDY, C.B., C.M.G., D.S.O.

References are to The History of the Great War, Military Operations, France and Belgium, Vols. I to V.

ARRANGEMENT OF REPORT

GENERAL REMARKS

PART I.—Tactical Lessons.
PART II.—Organization and Equipment.
PART III.—Training.

GENERAL REMARKS

The accompanying report is based on the study of the official History of the operations in France and Belgium in 1915-16, and on the personal experiences of a company, battalion, and brigade commander in France.

The study of these volumes leads to the conclusion that their most important lessons are concerned with " how not to do it ". The mistakes and failures recorded, it is now clear, were chiefly due to the inexperience of commanders, and the lack of training of the bulk of their troops.

The history (1915, p. 8) says: " For the British Leaders of all ranks the year 1915 was a period of education and instruction, it taught them the handling of hastily trained troops and improvized formations . . . " and on p. 291, " That greater success was not gained was as much due to faulty tactical direction from the General Staff . . ."

If this picture of the conditions is accepted as true, the question arises—how came the commanders to need such education on the field of battle, and why were half-trained troops called on to undertake tasks beyond their competence?

The opinions which I here venture to give must, from the nature of my experience, be unavoidably tinged with a " front line " mentality, which perhaps over-emphasises details coming within its narrow point of view. But this view-point has the advantage of comprising a complete, and for me ineffaceable, picture of the grim reality of battle, which the reading of the History brings again vividly to mind. For those without such experience, neither the stirring narrative of this History, nor

C

the colder precepts of the F.S.R., still less the make-believe of peace manœuvres, can ever produce the atmosphere of a fight like Delville Wood, or the deadly weariness of the swamps of Passchendaele.

The History shows that it is in the Battle, either in attack or defence, that the main weakness in leadership was shown. And today the training manuals, and the exercises based on them, can teach the army to " make war ", to reach and deploy on the battlefield, to stage a set-piece; but after that, the fighting troops are left very much to their own devices, as regards the conduct of the battle—which is " the decisive act in war ". (F.S.R., II, Sec. 21 (I).)

There is a school of thought which proposes that battle may be evaded by mobility, and war decided in some other way, especially if the enemy is " second class " and inert.

The power of the machine gun, with its modern mobile mounting, must be realized; so long as an enemy who is brave and determined is armed with such a weapon, and knows how to use it, he cannot be considered as " second class ". " Open war ", so-called, assumed to be won by superior rapidity of movement rather than by superior fire, may become possible when the nations are partially disarmed; but until then, and until some completely satisfactory answer to the machine gun is found, I believe that battles will be stabilized by fire and that more than mobility and manœuvre will be necessary to win them.

My report deals almost entirely with the Battle; the volumes in question being chiefly concerned with battles of " penetration ". There is, first, the attempted " break-in "; as here described, a deliberate, organized and unhurried " set piece ", which is reproduced, as far as possible, in our training exercises and manuals. Next the " break-through ", the " Battle of the broken front "; an elusive achievement, which today needs our careful attention. Partial, not complete success, is, it seems, the normal in war; and it is in describing the conditions accompanying a partial success that the manuals appear to be vague and even misleading. Our training can hardly hope to reproduce these conditions, if they are not recognized as the commonest characteristic of warfare.

A typical sentence may be quoted from the History, in this connection:—

" The Germans were able to get their machine guns out of the dug-outs, when our men were half way across No Man's Land."

This small detail—a matter of minutes, perhaps lost to consideration in the staging of a great battle—could neutralize the skilfully ordered approach march and deployment of an army, and cause its bloody defeat in the last few hundred yards.

If the subsequent notes are mainly in the form of criticism, it is that I am only trying to bring out the lessons which were not learnt, or not applied, in the War, and have perhaps been partly forgotten since. The great difficulties of our commanders no one appreciates more than I do; and I fully realize that they had few, if any, equals among our opponents. Wisdom after the event, however, must be applied to our training; in which, in the absence of fire, fear and the unknown—dominating factors in war—we are so prone to create unreal conditions. With this object, and not to construct theories and principles, I have tried to recapture some of the atmosphere of actual war, and to suggest improvements in the methods of waging it.

Briefly, the great lesson appears to be this:—that commanders, and, of course, their subordinates, trained only in the ordered system of peace, cannot quickly or easily adapt their ideas and outlook to the confusion, uncertainty and " fog " of war. War itself is its own school; but much can be done, and more, I think, than at present, to reproduce in our peace training at least some approximation to those conditions.

In his Preface, pp. VI and VII, the Historian says—" Its very misfortunes and mistakes make 1915 particularly worthy of study. In the remembrance of the final victory we are apt to forget the painful and weary stages by which it was reached, and the heavy cost in our best lives during these stages . . .

. . . Too many of the bravest and best perished, seeking to compensate by valour for lack of experience . . ."

A terrible price to pay—the history tells how it was paid by the British Army. It is surely our duty to endeavour to ensure that it shall never pay such a price again.

The Official History, 1915, p. 49—suggests that —" The unreadiness for a great war was not the fault of the Army and Navy, or of any department or officer of State, but was the consequence of the want of forethought of the whole body of British electors, their representatives and their Ministers . . . The whole spirit of the country was opposed to preparations for a great war ".

It was not so much opposed, as entirely incapable of believing that any great war could happen; and, in spite of bitter experience, the same spirit, though to a much less extent, persists today.

The chapters in the History dealing with the training and equipping of the National Army should be prescribed as a study for all military officers; and a great part of them might be used as material lessons to be embodied in the manuals.

The raising of our National Army, and its placing in the field in a form to be a worthy opponent (" ebenburtiger Gegner ") of the German Army, was the outstanding achievement of the War—one that many high professional authorities

C 2

amongst our enemies had declared impossible. But it is well to realize the cost of our period of unreadiness. The old army disappeared while the new army was being raised; it was said that the one never saw the other. The question of readiness for war remains a national one.

PART I.—TACTICAL LESSONS

1. *Difficulty of command in battle*

" In the open warfare of old days it was necessary to make beforehand a decision of the nature now called for . . . . with masses of men now engaged on a wide front under modern conditions, with communications unreliable and slow. A commander cannot take advantage of fleeting opportunities, he does not hear of them till too late, accordingly he leaves initiative to subordinate commanders and can only influence the battle by sending reserves."

Thus the History. It is only too easy to criticise the commanders, who were faced with difficulties new to them, often without means of coping with them. We should rather study those difficulties, and see how our manuals and our training prepare us to meet them in future.

It is clear that " command " became dislocated, as soon as a " break-in " had been made. So that, until success is complete, or failure final, the difficult conditions of the " broken front " will persist both for attack and defence. How to retain control, or exercise command, when communications are destroyed, fronts ragged, units intermixed, their losses and fighting value unknown, and the enemy's rear positions not located, is indeed a problem.

" This breaking of all communications with the front line battalions by the German bombardment, and the time (two or three hours) taken by runners to get back with the reports, made it difficult for corps and divisional commanders to take any action; their task was further complicated by the inaccuracy of some of the reports, chiefly due to the difficulty of picking up landmarks."

All these difficulties will continue to be present as consequences of the original operations; even if, as at Neuve Chapelle, almost completely successful. Only some unexpected, unlikely demoralization of the enemy can justify attempts to continue one successful operation by another, for which no adequate preparation has yet been made. Such demoralization, after one initial reverse on a limited front, will not overtake a good enemy.

Commanders must know how to control and influence the " broken battle ", with its uncertainties, fluctuations, and surprises. They will find themselves wrestling with a live enemy and a practical problem, instead of a passive target and a text book of maxims. It is by their capacity to deal with the " broken battle " as it progresses that victory will be won.

It may be said that most of the mistakes criticised in these notes were corrected in the later stages of the war, and that the lessons have been learnt. Those, however, who did so learn have mostly passed on; and others, quite inexperienced, may have to take their place. It needed four years of war to make even our best leaders finished experts. Yet for those who may take part in another war, previous instruction and training must provide reminders of its realities; of such apparently simple things as getting orders out in time, realizing how difficult it is to get information—how important the building up of reserves—how numbers dwindle, and units melt away in battle.

There is no doubt that the army today does its best to keep abreast of modern developments; and that it fixes its eyes on the future, determined to be up-to-date. There still remains the test of war, to put the new conditions and the new weapons to the test. But in the History it is made clear that it was by no means in things of military novelty that the principal mistakes were made.

2. *The attack*

The History says: " Given that the front of attack was wide enough to make it impossible for the small local reserves of the defence to deal with the situation, success was shown to be a time problem, a question of whether a break-in—which with adequate artillery preparation, was always possible—could be converted into a ' break-through ' before the enemy could be certain of the point of attack, and rush reinforcements to it ".

F.S.R. seem to me to deal almost entirely with the " break-in " attack. Taken for granted are accurate reconnaissance, unbroken communications, full-strength units, and in fact all the conditions and advantages of the leisurely rehearsed, set-piece attack. In discussing action after a successful " break-through ", it is suggested that conditions will be similar to advanced guard fighting. This is very misleading; since in advanced guard fighting the enemy's intention is usually to retire to his main position, and bold attack may probably hasten his retirement. After a " break-through " attack, the defender, if stout-hearted, continues to fight it out for every back position; bold attacks, not carefully prepared, would be folly. I consider that there is no real similarity between the two stages of the attack, or the attitude the enemy is likely to adopt in them.

There is a tendency to over-emphasize that the great difficulty which the attack had to contend with was organized trench positions; and to assume that attacks on such positions are not likely to be made again, at least at the beginning of the next war, or not at all in what is styled " open war ". It is even assumed that trench warfare is a thing of the past, and not to be considered or discussed. I think that in this school of thought there are certain dangerous fallacies.

In the first place, it was not the actual trenches that held up our action, but the automatic weapons which they contained. Apart from entrenchments, other means can be found to conceal, and protect from bombardment, the defenders' machine guns: and an effective concealed defence, given the favourable conditions, can be quickly laid out. In the second place, well trained troops can dig themselves in thoroughly in a single night; it does not need a Hindenburg Line to make a very formidable defensive position. I do not believe the defence in future will expose itself to artillery observation and fire, or to tank attacks, in the same crudely obvious way as in the last war. A countryside that has not had all its natural cover obliterated, to my mind can offer almost as serious an attack proposition as any Hindenburg Line.

The real problem of the attack is, I believe, the " break-through " fighting, that follows a successful, or partly successful " break-in ". This is the " Battle of the Broken Front " —with broken units and broken communications.

F.S.R. II, Chapter VII, Sec. 75, considers the final " phases ". The manuals, and also our training are concerned with the opening phase, and the final phase; but they treat quite inadequately the vital phase of the "break-through", which is the battle itself. Though criticism is easy, it is, of course, very different to find the solution, how to handle the " broken " battle.

The value of reconnaissance in this phase is not sufficiently emphasised, or the time required to make it; it seems to be taken for granted that the enemy opposite will be located easily—whereas, on the contrary, the great difficulty of this fighting is to locate him, and especially his machine guns. Here concealment is the greatest strength of the defence.

Improved methods are necessary for the fighting of the " break-through ". Command exercised from a " dug-out " may be useless, since destroyed communications involve decentralization of command. Commanders should have an organized plan for this, and they must go and see their battle. Communication becomes personal; reserves must be organized into mobile, self-contained, " break-through " groups, capable of penetrating, of fighting an isolated action for hours, and having bold tactical objectives, to be attained by methods of infiltration. Commanders of " break-through " groups must be properly supplied with staff and equipment, and not have command suddenly thrust upon them without any organization through which it can be exercised.

F.S.R. is unsatisfactorily vague in dealing with the " break-through " phase. It is admitted that infantry, if it finds itself " hung-up ", will need more artillery support; but it is suggested that, failing this, it must seize opportunities to get forward with its own weapons. Good infantry will always seize opportunities; but to drive it forward when there are no opportunities, and no prospects of success, must lead to the heaviest losses, and result only in enhancing the morale of the defence.

The conditions of the " broken " battle will apply just as much to the organized attempts of tank formations to penetrate. It is too often assumed that, after the " break-in ", these fighting machines, unlike bodies of foot soldiers, will be able to continue their ordered advance without loss of speed or direction. It seems certain that the two-men tank units must tend to become widely dispersed, and must each then fight its own isolated battle. Under such conditions, ordinary men do not fight at their best or boldest; individual hesitations, doubts, and fears, quite as much as enemy fire or the general " fog of war ", must tend to produce the same " broken " battle as for others. It is also sometimes forgotten that, even if this raggedness of advance can be avoided, the enemy does not remain static, or wait for the development of the tank manœuvre, with which his own modern equipment will probably be competent to deal.

The latest war lesson of the Far East goes to show that the most modern equipment of an enemy may be paralyzed by physical obstacles, weather conditions, and the tenacity of a few brave men, even behind inadequate or improvized defences.

3. *Value of surprise in attack*

Our methods, of course, improved as the war went on; but there was very little variety in our attack. We were prone to stereotype, if only from year to year; the newest method, each spring, was for universal application. In many of the attacks recorded no effort whatever was made to effect surprise; yet, against the deadly power of modern weapons, surprise and concealment are nearly always essential to success.

Where surprise was achieved, the attacks were uniformly successful. The History gives a clear description of the recapture of the Bluff (Ypres sector, 1916), which was remarkable for the fact that some imagination was exercised and complete surprise effected. The taking of Metren in 1918 by the 9th

Division was another instance of a successful attack, surprise being effected by the use of smoke, of camouflage, and various other ruses.

It is difficult to particularize on surprise; I suggest that it should be more stressed in the manuals, and much more attempted in training schemes. No daylight attack which has not some element of surprise, or concealment, should be deemed to have succeeded, if the defender's intention is to hold on to his position.

As to concealment; it is remarkable how few attempts were made to attack at night. This, I think, was due to the fixed idea that the artillery must see, even if at the same time the enemy's machine gunners could see as well.

As an instance, the History records (2nd Ypres) a daylight attack which failed; " the price paid was very heavy, and no ground was gained that could not have been secured probably without any casualty, by a simple advance after dark, to which the open country lent itself ". And in the same operations, two instances of successful approach to the enemy's position, under cover of darkness, are recorded.

The History, in detailing the tactical instructions issued by G.H.Q. immediately before the Somme battle (1916), remarks that " the possibility of using night or dawn attacks in the course of the battle received no mention ".

The success of the attack on Longueval (14th July, 1916) was due to careful preparation and bold patrolling, which rendered the operation much less difficult.

Smoke screens may well be as useful as was the fog in March, 1918, to the German attacks, though considerable practice and experience are required to produce them effectively.

In the break-through fighting all the infantry ask is that there be enough shells fired to shake the enemy's nerve, obscure his view of the battlefield, and derange his fire. For this a weapon of the nature of the Stokes mortar, of simple machanism, would be most useful.

4. *Continuation of the attack, after partial success or failure*

The failure of the attempts to continue the attack, and exploit the initial success at Neuve Chapelle (1915), carried on during the second day's battle, was attributed, says the History, mainly to the difficulties of getting information back from the front line as to the position and extent of the new German trenches which had been dug overnight. The Army Command knew where its own troops were, but no more; and on this knowledge, orders were issued in accordance with the original plan—though this had proved, so far, to be incapable of fulfilment.

F.S.R. II, Sec. 74, para. 14, deals with a similar situation, but turns on the meaning of " effectively ". In the example above-quoted, penetration to the Aubers Ridge (the original objective) had not been effective; and persistence in the attack on it, without further preparation or reconnaissance, resulted in two days of useless slaughter.

This paragraph should be much enlarged, so that the difference between continuation of attack, and re-attack is made clearer. The correct action in case of partial penetration, as well as of complete failure, should be indicated. In all this fighting, there appears to be no clear cut distinction between the two cases.

Section 64 of the same chapter deals with the continuation of the attack, to my mind very inadequately; it gives no hint of the many difficulties and obstacles in the way of progression from one objective to the next (para. 11), and no idea of how the series of assaults (para. 11) are to be organized, when partial penetration has been achieved, and the complications of the battle of the " Broken front " arise. Minute air reconnaissance and the bold use of fighting patrols are essential at this stage.

In this connection, everything in the History points the lesson that, against an approximately equal enemy, no unorganized, improvised, secondary attacks can ever succeed.

From Chapter VII of F.S.R., and from a great deal of our training, the impression is got that such attacks can normally succeed. In the battle of Neuve Chapelle the commanders on both sides, on hearing of some local failure, felt it a point of honour to reverse it without delay, and regardless of the cause of failure, or the condition of their troops, or of their losses. Orders twenty-four hours old were considered applicable next morning to the movement of units, several of which had for the time ceased to exist, and most of which had lost forty or fifty per cent. One of the most important pieces of information a commander can have is the casualty list. About such a thing F.S.R. are silent, and the History all too full.

5. *Difficulties of the counter-attack*

To counter-attack successfully, either immediately the attack is stopped, or more deliberately, is in either case one of the most difficult operations of war. The immediate counter-attack has to overcome the difficulty, that the troops detailed for it, in order to be near at hand, must unavoidably be kept in the attack area. In my experience, the direction and control of these troops are very difficult. It is not easy actually to locate the enemy, and danger aften threatens from the flanks; in fact, the undertaking is often a pure gamble, and should be carried out only for some urgent reason, and never as a mere routine action of the defence.

Here of course, I am not considering the small counter-attacks of sections and platoons, which are part of the fighting in the position before capture.

The deliberate counter-attack is nothing but a re-attack, and should be treated as such. In the period covered by the History, counter-attack, the " retour offensive ", seems to have been looked upon as the inevitable reaction to the loss of position or ground, however valueless. In fact it had come to be considered by some commanders as being necessary to restore the " dash " of their own troops who had failed. The counter-attacks (2nd Ypres, 1915, and elsewhere), entailed heavy losses; and were generally launched for no sufficient reason, and with hardly the smallest prospect of success. Says the History—" In view of the ill success and heavy losses in the counter-attacks of the 80th and 84th Brigades, and in many others of the previous four weeks, made in haste with totally inadequate artillery backing, the decision come to by the 4th Division (i.e., not to counter-attack) appears to have been a thoroughly sound one. It was concurred in by all the officers at the front, and was fully in accord with the view held by the French brigade and battalion commanders who, like their forefathers of Crimean days, had for some time regarded the desperate counter-attacks made by the British as ' magnificent, but not war ' ".

F.S.R. II, Sec. 82, paras. 1 and 2, seem to me very vague and non-committal on this difficult question. It again gives no indication of the battlefield difficulties, nor any warning of what is the inevitable and heavy cost of failure. Particularly it does not even suggest that surprise is an essential to success.

Should not F.S.R. enter into the nature of the reasons influencing a commander to embark on this difficult operation, and give more space to discuss the conditions under which alone it is likely to succeed? I do not believe that there can be a hope of success for an immediate counter-attack in daylight, if more than a few hundred yards have to be covered. For a short distance pace and the bayonet are the two deciding factors.

The History shows that counter-attacks were often ordered by commanders having no conception of the actual state of affairs, nor yet how their orders were to be delivered, distributed, or carried out.

6. *Phases of the attack*

At Neuve Chapelle, and throughout the war, the first phase was most carefully rehearsed. We should, however, consider rather the unrehearsed phase, the impromtu fighting which follows the success, or partial success of the rehearsed. If the first phase, even when reheased, is only partially successful, we must surely expect the unrehearsed phases to be more difficult. F.S.R. II, Sec. 75, the only one to deal with these phases of the attack, regards them as " final " and throws no light on the subject.

It seems that the planning of a succession of phases on a map (in coloured lines) before the first phase has begun, must tend to produce unreality in the whole scheme, and certain disappointment in the results obtained. A second phase should at least be constructed on the foundation made by the troops in the first; and so on to the remaining phases. F.S.R. does not suggest this; nor in our training do we give the time, or practice, to the commander to construct his battle progressively. Our method has been to do all our reconstructing before the battle begins, with the result that commanders are often non-plussed when it fails to go according to plan. It is the making of new plans, to meet new developments which is the real test of a commander.

7. Plans conceived in accordance with accepted principles of war

F.S.R. II, Chap. I, Sec. 5. " To be effective the plan must be conceived in accordance with established principles of war, and with possibilities of available resources; it must be clearly explained, developed with imagination, tempered by reasoned judgment and carried out with resolution, intelligence and adaptability ". This would be the perfect plan; but the established principles, without which it would be worse than useless, are not so easily practised, or even distinguished.

The plan of the battle of Neuve Chapelle has already been alluded to, as a set-piece, in which no established principles appeared to be violated. The History gives a good example, however, of an attack. (2nd Ypres, 1915) described as " Hull's attack ", in which both the troops and their actual leader, were called upon to make an attempt which was contrary to elementary rules.

" The men exhausted and reduced in numbers by previous fighting were called on to attempt the impossible. Without adequate artillery support and preparation, on ground unknown and unreconnoitred, they were sent to turn an enemy well provided with machine-guns out of a position which had ready-made cover in houses and a wood, and splendid artillery observations from higher ground behind it."

This is, of course, an extreme example; yet the orders for the attack came from members of a professional, highly trained staff, such as it was in 1915. I only quote this as an example of the deterioration which may be expected sometimes to occur in an inexperienced command, under the strain which the conditions of the battle impose. Our endeavour should be to ensure that the effects of this strain are not to fight blindly, without a plan, trusting to the valour of the troops to save the siuation. There are limits to what even the bravest troops in the world can achieve.

Again, says the History: " The losses of the 10th Brigade in its magnificent but hopeless attempt had been heavy, totalling 73 officers and 2,346 other ranks, mostly irreplaceable, well-trained men. In compensation for the disaster that had overtaken them, the battalions had the satisfaction of knowing later that they had stopped any possible enemy advance in the St. Julien quarter . . . ". Probably an intelligent use of bullets instead of bodies might have achieved the same result. It is a question whether we have yet sufficiently studied the possibility of the attack by fire, for both holding and counter-attack.

8. *The holding attack*

It would appear from the History that a holding attack was conceived as merely an ordinary attack, from which not only all attempt at surprise has been eliminated, but which was to be made as obvious to the enemy as possible.

In the Somme battle (1916)—" The attempt ' to divert against itself forces ' which might otherwise ' be directed against the left flank of the main attack near Serre ', cost the VII Corps nearly seven thousand casualties ". And again, " In consequence of the nature of the operation the VII Corps with Sir Douglas Haig's approval made no attempt to hide or disguise the preparation for the attack ". And the corps commander, asked whether his preparations had been noticed by the enemy, replied—" they know we are coming all right ".

There seems to be nothing in F.S.R., or anywhere else on the subject. Surely it needs to be most carefully thought out; and every endeavour should be made to indicate how a holding attack need not be an inevitable and useless sacrifice of men's lives. Cannot attack by fire be further exploited? Need the same forces, in the same formations, be used, as for a main attack? Surely here strong fighting patrols could have kept the enemy employed? I cannot believe that the morale of any troops in the world will stand, knowingly, exposure to such treatment.

9. *Difficulty of intercommunication in battle*

The History stresses the breaking of all communication with the front line (Neuve Chapelle, 1915) by the enemy's artillery bombardment. Without communication, command cannot function; it can neither receive information, nor get out its orders. The army is then fighting without a brain; or worse still, with a disordered brain which acts regardless of reality. In the manuals and in our training we take perfect communications for granted; or if they are deranged, we assume we can carry on all the same. I suggest that the elaborately perfect communications of the approach, deployment, and initial attack cannot be maintained, indeed would be quite unsuitable for the " broken front " fighting; we should consider other and simpler methods.

To begin with, our plans in the " break-through " fighting should be based on the possible minimum of intercommunication. Commanders must realize that troops once launched into the fighting, so far as they themselves are concerned, are troops expended, who must perforce be left to fight forward as far as they can.

The higher command should, therefore, trust to self-reliant subordinate leaders to carry on the immediate battle, and concern itself with the use of the reserves for extending the operations. The atmosphere of peace training inspections, and the constant question—" why don't you do something ", tend, I believe, to produce a habit of nervous activity in our commanders; a habit which may be translated into the " Hurry turmoil, and shadow of defeat " so frequently depicted in the pages of the History.

If we would devote more attention in our training to the value of patience, of coolness, and of waiting on developments, we could give communications and information the opportunity and time to work as they should in action. Commanders would then have a chance to exercise constructive ability; and training might even produce some more real picture of the long and desperate struggle of a modern battle.

As regards the actual system of communication, the elaborate back area system is quite unsuitable for the real battlefield. Here the chief means of communication are motor bicycles, horses, or runners. Infantry especially could act far more efficiently if fully equipped with motor bicycles. There is, however, good prospect that the real solution will be found in wireless. No cost would be too great that ensured to the brain of the army its full influence in the battle.

There is room in our training for developing a good deal more " signal sense " in all ranks. It should be second nature to every young commander to think it terms of signalling when making his plan; yet, in my experience, he seldom does so. He must learn, too, particularly to economize in signallers, and to appreciate the difference between what is important, in messages, and what is not. In the regiment, in my opinion, the signallers are too much a class apart. If communication is to be improved, the signallers must " join the army ".

10. *Information*

The whole two volumes (1915-16) abound in instances of lack of information, or of information completely erroneous; and, under real fighting conditions, this is not surprising. But commanders should not be encouraged to act without information; the maxim that, in war, " to do something, even if wrong, is better than to do nothing " needs much qualification. Alert inactivity is better than rash, costly activity for the sake of action alone. The key to all successful leadership is this knowing when to hold the hand, to examine things and get information before acting.

The manuals do not deal with the " broken battle ", and perhaps can hardly do so in their limited compass. Training however, could give much more attention to it. The tendency is to permit important, or vital information to pass through too many centres. The History shows how reports, having filtered through various subordinate headquarters, reached the Army Commander at Merville in a very misleading form. There is nothing strange in this; each forwarding agency added its own ideas to what is collected, and these ideas became less and less related to facts the further they travelled. The only staffs to get the real truth, or part of it, were the brigade staffs, and if they could have communicated direct with the Army Commander, he might have formed a much more accurate picture. It might even be possible in an emergency to eliminate intermediate agencies, or serve them with reports later; so that the commander should get direct messages from those in the actual battle, and get them early. There are obvious disadvantages in such an arrangement, no doubt; these, however, might still not outweigh the disadvantages of situations, so common in this History, where the commander, forming his conception from false premises, issues orders incapable of fulfilment, or capable of making a bad situation far worse.

For collecting information as to the course of a battle, no one is so well placed as a looker-on. The fighting man is too busy, and his horizon is too narrow; generally the attempt to enlarge this horizon, under fire, can only result in his ceasing to be a source of information himself. The independent, roving information patrol should be more used.

At both ends of the battle, officers should learn to make economy in messages the rule; they cannot expect a tape machine in a battle.

Do we study means of accurately identifying our own troops, in these days when many other armies have copied our uniform? Of course, some of the methods suggested during the war did not commend themselves to the front-line troops. Troops who have with great difficulty captured a position, can, for example, hardly be expected to invite enemy bombardment, by indulging in any sort of fireworks for the information of their own airmen.

The manuals do not lay much stress on the importance of information about the position of our own troops during the battle. In training, of course, this information is constantly available; but in war (as the History brings out clearly) the command usually knows little either of the actual location, or of the physical conditions of its own men. If their situation is bad, or their state unfavourable for further exertions, there is no use in the commander attempting to strike a decisive blow with a weapon that may break in his hand. As an example of ignorance of the situation, the History relates (2nd Ypres, 1916) how an attack, planned to be undertaken by fifteen battalions, was really carried out by five battalions.

11. *Orders*

For operation orders, and instructions, appendices 11, 18 and 20 to Vol. III of the official History are very instructive. The First Army operations order, No. 9, cannot, however, be properly read without the " special instructions " issued to corps commanders.

The First Army operations order No. 9 was followed some 24 hours later by No. 11 (what intervened between these two the History does not say), and 24 hours later again by No. 12. Both No. 11 and No. 12, ordered the troops to do what they had failed to do on the 10th March; *i.e.*, to capture the Aubers Ridge position. It must have been increasingly evident that they could not do this; in fact the History shows that brigade and division commanders frankly recognized the impossibility, and even went so far as to point it out. Was there, in spite of this, a neglect, or reluctance to inform Army Headquarters of the real situation? Or, being duly informed, did the Army Headquarters think that sufficiently strongly worded orders would produce a result that otherwise could not be achieved? The History cites a wire from the Army Commander:—" Information indicates that enemy on our front *are much demoralized*. Indian Corps and IV Corps will push through the barrage of fire *regardless of loss*, using reserves if required". How could any enemy whose " barrage of fire " might entail severe losses and the use of reserves be described as " demoralized "?

F.S.R. might, on this subject of orders, include a note to the effect that such phrases as " at all costs ", " regardless of loss ", or " to the last man " should never be used in orders, however appropriate they may be when used by a company commander, who is himself going to be part of the sacrifice. British troops need not, ordinarily, be told to do their duty in face of the enemy; and to ask them to do it, in orders that may perhaps fall into the enemy's hands or come somehow into his knowledge, can only encourage his resistance. At the same time, the notion that a highly trained and efficient enemy is to be " demoralized " by a partial reverse, of the kind at Neuve Chapelle, should be eradicated from every soldier's mind; it is part of that most dangerous of all mental attitudes in war—despising the enemy.

The time allowed, not only for orders to reach units, but for units to digest them and issue their own orders, and act upon them, was, according to the History, frequently insufficient. The IV Corps orders (Neuve Chapelle, 1915) sent out on the 10th March at 2.55 p.m. were for an advance at 3.30 p.m.—thirty-five minutes, under battle conditions, to get every battalion concerned informed and in motion. In the result, the attack began disjointedly about 5 p.m., in gathering darkness. The paragraphs of F.S.R. dealing with this matter should emphasize strongly that sooner than allow too little time for orders to be mastered by the recipients, it would be better to give double the time, and so allow ample margin for delays and miscarriages.

The result of the deliberate methods of fighting in the last war was to encourage the writing of orders that were much too long and elaborate. A great factor in the speeding-up of our operations will be a habit of getting the essential orders out in the shortest possible time.

On the 21st March, 1918, I asked a captured German " storm " trooper, what his orders were. He replied " So weiter, so besser ". As these four words had taken him through nearly to my brigade H.Qs. they had been remarkably effective.

12. Defence

F.S.R. II, Chap. VIII, Sec. 77 (3). " Defensive positions however strong are of no value unless the defenders have the courage and determination to defend them to the last, and the skill to make full use of their weapons."

The History (1915, Neuve Chapelle) says—" the enemy showed, as the British troops had shown at Ypres, the tremendous value of a few brave men holding on in strong points and isolated trenches ". It is well to remember that it is defenders rather than defences which make the strength of a position; without them it is merely an obstacle, at most a cause of a temporary delay.

The regulations seem to lay considerable emphasis on the increased difficulty in attack, as defences become more elaborate. On the other hand our training too often gives the impression that, in the absence of such elaborate defences, hastily mounted and badly supported attacks may succeed. Yet it is only necessary to read the history of the Ypres " Salient ", to realize that the most stubborn resistance was often made in the ruins of such defences as remained.

" It was the spirit of ' ils ne passeront pas ', rather than elaborate fortifications, that held Verdun. Again, as I personally know, the British Army held no highly organized position on Wytschaete Ridge, when it received Sir Douglas Haig's famous " our backs to the wall " message.

In the battle of manœuvre it is organized defenders, rather than organized defences, which we should chiefly consider.

F.S.R. II, Chap. VIII, Sec. 80 (2).—" The first consideration will be to determine what ground is vital to the battle. This decision having been made the defensive position will be selected."

This sound principle was almost forgotten in the period under review. Both armies seemed to have been obsessed with the fetish of not giving up ground. No doubt political reasons determined the holding on to Ypres, and the " Salient " but it is impossible to understand the determination to hang on to every inch, or to incur ruinous losses in attempting to regain every yard lost.

13. *Machine guns*

F.S.R. II, Chap. VIII, Sec. 83 (6), states—" As long as machine guns are holding out, no position can be regarded as lost.".

This is absolutely true; it is the other side of the picture of the " break-through " fight, already discussed.

In the hurry of our peace-time training, it is essential that the effect of the machine gun which is fought to the last in defence, is not lost to sight. We need to instil the " will to win " just as much in defence as in attack. To maintain a high morale in the defence is certainly much harder than in the attack, at least in the early stages. Our training is too apt to allow attack to succeed. Defence becomes accustomed to defeat—and confidence in the power of modern defence is undermined.

14. *Defence: the use of surprise*

F.S.R. II, Chap. VIII, Sec. 78 (3). " Surprise is just as important in the defence as in the attack. In selecting a position for defence, a commander must consider what facilities are offered for concealing his dispositions . . .".

Surprise, chiefly attained by the concealment of the defender's dispositions, is of primary importance. With the great elaboration of defences in the war, nearly all attempts at concealment were given up. Yet, as I have pointed out, the

D

most stubborn defence was often made in shell holes, and in remains of ruined defences, because the defenders and their positions were then hidden.

Without referring to the History, memory will recall so many " snag trenches "—like the famous " snag trench " in front of the Butte de Warlencourt—just a simple trench which was so placed behind a little rise, that no one could see it. Time after time the most carefully prepared, heavily supported, and determined attacks broke down as they topped the slight ridge in front of it; because not a single hit had been made on it. Incidents like this are not easily forgotten.

In a war of manœuvre there will probably be no extensive, obvious and elaborate defence systems to be battered down. There will be many surprises, and many " snag trenches " to be dealt with; we must practice both the art of making these ourselves, and of being prepared for the sudden opposition offered by those of the enemy. Concealment is the secret of the power of small arms in defence.

Surprise can often be effected by movement. The defences in the last war were as rigid as they were obvious. There were, however, some occasions used (chiefly by the Germans) to arrange a defence by moving outposts, or posts which were frequently varied. An example was the period (1918) just before the British attack on Meteren; when such dispositions by the Germans were a source of anxiety to those planning the British attack. No doubt the defence may be worried, and its plans hindered, if it has posts in front of its main position; but a sufficiently flexible fire plan should ensure the necessary variation and fluidity in this form of defence.

15. *Use of reserves*

(a) In attack.—F.S.R. II, Chap.VII, Sec. 83 (3). " A commander exercises his influence in the subsequent course of the operation by his organization of fire and by the use of his reserves."

Here the regulations are quite sound. But in practice the successful use of reserves was of rare occurrence. There developed a tendency, with limited objectives and " leap frog " methods, to commit reserves to a certain rôle before operations began. It should be laid down clearly that troops committed to a definite rôle at any state of the battle have ceased to be a reserve; a reserve should be free of any commitment. This commitment of reserves, so frequently made, was part of the tendency to plan the whole battle beforehand, to trust to the preconceived idea, and to mistrust any constructive thinking as the battle progressed.

(*b*) In defence.—F.S.R. II, Chap. VIII, Sec. 81, etc.—
Nowhere do the regulations seem to contemplate defensive
fighting such as occurred at Ypres and on numerous other
occasions.

The History (1915, 2nd Ypres) says—" The higher leaders
rarely had more than vague data on which to form a plan, and
the only course open to them was to supply the subordinate
leaders on the spot with the means, in the shape of reinforcements, to influence the combat " . . . " The control by higher
commanders of the actual fighting when once it had begun
remained almost negligible . . . ".

Thus it gives the impression that the throwing of all
available reserves piecemeal into the chaos, as reinforcements,
was inevitable.

I do not think such an idea can be entertained for a moment.
It would have been much better to lose a great deal of the
ground which at Ypres, for example, was so stubbornly contested, than to lose control of the reserves. Ground that merely
swallows up men—or a defence which only expends the
defenders—such things serve no useful purpose. Reserves in
hand are the only means by which the commander can influence
the battle.

It appears, from the History, that reserves were constantly
and extravagently expended in answer to any call or sign of
distress. Both the regulations, and our training, should
emphasize the fact that a commander with no reserves at his
disposal ceases to be a commander at all. In fact a great part
of the training of our future commanders should be concerned
with this problem of handling reserves in battle.

16. *The study of success*

The History (1915, 2nd Ypres) says—" This was one of
those fine feats in defence of which, because it was so entirely
successful there is little to be said, except that the accuracy of
British musketry told ".

It seems important to study more than we do the reasons
underlying " unobtrusive " successes. They are inclined to be
taken for granted, perhaps because defeat or failure attracts
more attention and its causes are more obvious.

I have personally observed the extraordinarily different
results obtained by units attacking side by side; but success was
usually ascribed to luck, or a poor enemy, while failure
attracted attention by reason of its clumsy and bloody struggle.
But a careful study would probably reveal that better methods
and more intelligent leadership were the reasons for the success
that seemed so easy, and it is these methods that best repay
study.

D 2

PART II.—ORGANIZATION AND EQUIPMENT

The History (1915, Preface) says—" It is to 1915 rather than to 1914, or the later years of the war that we must look for lessons as regards raising troops, organizing munitions supply and conducting operations with newly formed divisions ". And again—" too many of the bravest and best perished, seeking to compensate by valour for lack of experience and the shortage of munitions, to the hazard of the final victory and the detriment of the future of the nation ".

One of the most important lessons to be learnt should be how we are to expand our small army for the purposes of war; so as to avoid the initial sacrifice of our trained officers and men, who are irreplaceable.

Another is to realize, when we have so expanded it, what a new army of the kind is capable of achieving.

There is a tendency to aim at a very high standard of training for our small nucleus of a regular army; to load it with a complicated armament, to train it in the use of wide formations, which need skilled leadership and expert personnel, and to think in terms of rapid and accurate manœuvre.

If too high a standard is aimed at, there is a danger that a veneer may be cultivated at the expense of sound and thorough training; and that tactical theories may be adopted which the less highly trained armies of war time may be incapable of putting into execution.

One of the main causes of the disorder in the Fifth Army in 1918 was that an untrained army was obliged to attempt a difficult manœuvre in retreat, in which it had never been instructed or exercised. As brigade-commander of a " Kitchener " brigade, I was the only man in it who knew how to get back to the next position, while in contact with the advancing enemy.

We need to ask—what are our present, or contemplated arrangements for raising and training troops for another war, for organizing supplies, etc., or for using these troops in the field? Do we now understand the military limitations of such new troops? Or is it intended that they are again to be used for purposes for which they are not fitted, in the attempting of which they must certainly fail.

Equipment.—The weight carried by the infantry soldier needs no reference from the History; I am aware that it is under constant discussion. When it comes to be considered what is necessary, it is well to remember that once in action many soldiers discarded a great deal of their original load, and yet were able to continue fighting.

There is not much satisfaction, when you have failed because you were too slow, in knowing how excellently you were equipped for success.

The entrenching tool.—The experiences of the war prove conclusively that no troops who have not some means of throwing up hasty protection will be able to maintain themselves on a modern battlefield.

In the fight with machine guns the spade becomes almost as valuable as the rifle and its use is a tactical operation, not a " fatigue ".

High-explosive shell.—My experience was that H.E. was much more effective under most conditions than shrapnel. As a barrage I found it much easier to follow, and much more deadly to face than shrapnel.

There is no comparison between the two, in the moral effect on infantry.

PART III.—TRAINING

The History (1915, Preface) says—" It is quite impossible to describe on paper—as for instance the Battle of Waterloo can be described—the organized confusion of modern warfare ".

The same impossibility limits the usefulness of training manuals; they can never produce a picture of modern war. Most of such lessons as a theoretical treatise can embody are sufficiently set out in the manuals; if we are to look for improvement, it must be chiefly in our training. This must be directed to teaching the practical application of the theory of the manuals to the varying conditions and situations of war. Since the last war our system and method of training have greatly improved, especially in endeavours to introduce a certain realism in our exercises. It is, therefore, not for the sake of mere criticism that I offer the following remarks.

1. *Training of subordinate leaders*

F.S.R. II, Chap. I, Secs. 3 and 4. " Success largely depends on the decision of subordinate leaders who therefore must be always ready to accept responsibility."

Does our training encourage self-reliance and initiative in the subordinate leaders? As the war progressed, the tendency grew for the subordinate leader to be given practically no responsibility in the opening stage of a battle. Detailed orders prescribed his action in minute detail, with the result that a standardized army might go into a standardized battle. Once the battle became " broken ", the leading strings broke too, the responsibility became spread about; till, after a time, it became customary to speak of " a platoon commander's war ".

It is essential that the daily life of an officer should offer opportunities, for acquiring the habits of self-reliance and of accepting responsibilities; if these qualities are left to lie dormant, it must not be expected that they will be ready for production in emergency.

Have the standardization and rigid control from above, which became necessary as the war progressed and the army changed, been sufficiently relaxed. Are we prepared to leave his methods of command and training to the choice of the young officer, and to judge him on results?

2. *Training programme*

Training is inclined to be rigid and follow a set programme year by year, regardless of varieties of locality and climate, and of changed personnel. Thus we sometimes find an officer fresh from the excellent, highly organized training at Aldershot, confidently producing the same programme at Lucknow, where all the conditions are different. But he has standardized his programme, and it has become one of his most cherished possessions. As a paper programme it may be a model, and yet, for practical purposes of training under new conditions, quite useless.

Unfortunately, many people prefer to use their memory rather than their brains. We look up what was done last year; quote the remarks of some expert we have served under, perhaps slightly alter one of his schemes, and persuade ourselves it is our own.

It is essential in training to encourage originality and the assumption of responsibility on the part of young officers. If by so doing the training of the rank and file may suffer at first, this will be more than compensated by the discovery and training of self-reliant commanders of the future, on whom more than any other thing our success will depend.

3. *Control of training exercises*

The modern system of umpiring is a great advance in trying to simulate war conditions in peace training. Even, however, with the best umpire staff, it is difficult to prevent interest in the actual movement of troops from predominating over interest in imaginary fire conditions, which should hinder the same. Time can seldom be spared to let fire develop effectively, either in attack or defence. Perhaps some artificial time system such as makes so many hours " elapse " during presentation of a play, might be devised. But the element of time is most essential to the exercise of command, to the use of communications, and the collecting and passing of information. Our exercises often go so fast, that all these vital parts of the system of command are expected to work under conditions impossible for their free development.

4. *Manœuvres*

Manœuvres are the most practical form of training for command; they introduce the human element, and the many practical difficulties which are associated with its presence.

Every effort is, I believe, now made by experienced leaders to introduce a war atmosphere; but even so there is still a tendency to deal too much with the opening phases of an operation, and to make the general conditions of it too easy.

More attention might be given to the " broken battle "; and more time and practice in handling reserves.

The situations for the commanders to deal with might produce more variety—giving scope for quick and decisive action, as well as for more deliberate, constructive planning. We need versatile commanders, who can react to the infinitely varying conditions of battle.

5. *Night operations*

The paucity of instances, in the History (1915-16) of attempts to use the cover of night for operation is very remarkable. The main objections to so using it seem to have been, firstly, that there could be no artillery observation, and, secondly, that night operations are very difficult, and can only be carried out, against a limited objective, by a comparatively small force.

This is all true; but darkness is cover, just as much as is artillery fire—and is very helpful in effecting surprise.

If more attention were paid to night operations in our training we should develop a night sense, and many of the alleged difficulties would then disappear.

Of course there are strict limitations to operation by night; but as a means of approach to a strongly defended position, night advance and attack should occupy a prominent place in our training.

6. *Training the war army*

The official History (1916. General remarks) quotes a German official monograph (Somme—Nord) as saying—" The British Army . . . in the battle of the Somme had not yet reached a sufficiently high tactical standard. The training of the infantry was clearly behind that of the German; the superficially trained British were particularly clumsy in movements of large masses . . . The officers . . . went ahead of their men in battle with great courage. But, owing to insufficient training, they were not skilful in action ".

This criticism and appreciation of our army in 1916, by the enemy, seems very fair.

It is interesting to consider the action of a mechanized, mobile, quick-striking force, which will undoubtedly be most effective. But unless extraordinarily successful in the opening battles (in which it will probably meet another mechanized army), we may again be forced to fall back on a hastily trained national army. In this case perhaps some better machinery can be devised, to turn out an army of a higher standard; but if not, it is all-important that we should study the capabilities and limitations of a national army.

Does our training include sufficient study of what these " masses " of half-trained troops can be asked to do; or the formations and manœuvre best suited to exploit their magnificent natural qualities?

CONCLUSION

The study of this period of the last war, in France and Belgium, brings out all the difficulties to be overcome in battles between forces of high morale, and first class equipment. It was a period in which the defence had established superiority over the attack; and this superiority was due, partly to the power and accuracy of modern weapons, and partly to the fact that, with flanks secured against any possible manœuvres, nothing was possible but frontal attacks.

I do not intend to suggest in my report, that such conditions will always persist. I feel sure, on the contrary, that, in the class of major operations which our training contemplates, manœuvre and mobility will play a leading part; and good commanders find, and know how to grasp, those fleeting opportunities which, if rightly used, can turn partial success into complete victory. I know, too, that the problems of such operations are being studied, and applied in our training; and that there is no need to stress further what is already in our manuals. What these latter, of course, cannot picture, nor our training produce, are the real conditions of warfare—the disorder that must be controlled to make manœuvre possible—the confusion that hampers mobility—or the shells and bullets under which opportunity dies.

It was lack of experience and appreciation of these conditions which confounded our commanders in the last war. The next war will, no doubt, be different from the last; yet all wars entail fighting, for which capable and experienced commanders are very necessary. In our peace-time studies of the " war of manœuvre ", we must not forget the sordid details of the actual man-to-man struggles, which so often made manœuvre possible. The most important object of our training must be to produce commanders with the character and ability to turn unfamiliar conditions to their own advantage, and who will neither be crushed by the unexpected, nor afraid of the unknown.

(Sd.) J. R. KENNEDY,
Major-General.

APPENDIX III

REPORT ON THE LESSONS FROM THE MILITARY OPERATIONS IN GALLIPOLI BY LIEUT.-GENERAL W. M. ST. G. KIRKE, C.B., C.M.G., D.S.O.

References quoted are to the History of the Great War, Military Operations, Gallipoli, Vols. I and II

ARRANGEMENT OF REPORT

PART I.—Peace preparations.
PART II.—Stategy and Tactics.
PART III.—Organization and Equipment.
PART IV.—Peace training.

PART I.—PEACE PREPARATIONS AND ORGANIZATION

Staff at the War Office must not be changed on mobilization

1. The principal causes of failure of the campaign as a whole were divided counsels and consequent vacillation at the directing-head.

This was due mainly to the want of an authoritative study of the requirements of the campaign, on which the Cabinet could base a decision with all the material facts at its disposal. (Vol. I, p. 30.)

This again may be traced to want of confidence on the part of the Secretary of State in the general staff machine at his disposal, and to a failure of all the authorities concerned to make any use of it (Vol. I, Preface iii, pp. 46, 47, 69 (footnote), Vol. II, p. 378).

Far more reliance would have been placed in the trained general staff which, unfortunately, was removed overseas at the outbreak of war.

Later on, the general staff regained its rightful position in the councils of the Empire.

The lesson is that the personality of the C.I.G.S. and the confidence reposed in him by the Government are of paramount importance. He should not be moved on mobilization, and since he cannot function without a thoroughly trained and efficient staff, the members of the latter must also remain at their posts.

The very natural anxiety of the specially selected officers at the War Office to get to the front as soon as possible renders the mistake peculiarly liable to recur on a future occasion.

The method adopted later in the war, by which officers with recent knowledge of the different fronts were periodically brought home to replace others at the War Office, was undoubtedly the correct one, as combining continuity of work with up-to-date knowledge of practical conditions in the various theatres of war.

The system of liaison officers, travelling between the War Office and the various fronts, also proved its value when first class officers were employed.

The importance of a National Government immediately war becomes probable

2. The fall of the Liberal Government, and its replacement by a National Government, took place just at a time when the initial attacks on the Peninsula had failed both at Krithia and Anzac. It was then vitally important to take a major decision as to reinforing the M.E.F., or withdrawing it altogether.

During this inter-regnum there was no one to make this decision, with th result that the Turks were given yet more time for counter-preparations. (Vol. I, p. 365, Vol. II, p. 7.)

The formation of a National Government on mobilization would have avoided this unfortunate occurrence.

Necessity for joint study by the services in peace of all possible operations

3. Prior to 1914, and in spite of the Committee of Imperial Defence which carried out invaluable work in co-ordinating the mobilization of the fighting services and civil departments, the war plans of the fighting services themselves were not in unison.

Even in 1914, after the outbreak of war, we find the First Sea Lord making preparations for combined operations in the Baltic, which the General Staff would have considered to be militarily impossible (Vol. I, p. 49 and Soldiers and Statesmen, p. 83), the C.-in-C. on the Western front pressing for a landing on the coast of Belgium, whilst the First Lord and others were anxious to force the Dardanelles and capture Constantinople. The last named eventually carried the day, more or less fortuitously, but they did not, unfortunately, carry with it all the other directors of the business.

The disastrous changes of plan from a predominantly military operation to a purely naval attack on the forts, finally changing back again into a military operation, when all element of surprise had been dissipated, can be traced to lack of a reasoned pronouncement by the combined staffs. Moreover, the enterprise was eventually initiated without the General Staff having formulated any plan; indeed they were not even informed by the then C.I.G.S. of the Government's decision until nearly a month after that decision had been taken. (Vol. I, p. 69, footnote.)

One result was that the transports were loaded for disembarkation in a friendly harbour. (Vol. I, 109, *et seq.*)

The increased resisting power of small detachments, and improved communications, render the most careful preparation of " Combined operations " more than ever necessary. The M.E.F. was short of almost everything—ammunition, signals, R.E. stores of all kinds. (Vol. I, p. 119, *et seq.*) Moreover, the officers and men of both services had had little, if any, previous training in this most difficult of all questions.

There are many peace stations—the Mediterranean, Singapore, North Ireland, Scotland, the Coast of India, etc.—where little training other than combined operations is possible in peace time. It is for consideration whether we take sufficient advantage of our opportunities in this respect.

It is also open to question whether the system laid down in the " Manual of Combined Operations, 1931 " (Sec. 9) of equality of command as between the three services is workable in practice. History teems with examples where it failed with only two services in question, the most recent example perhaps being the abortive attack on Tanga.

It is suggested that if there is a properly worked out plan, as there should be, the Government which initiates the operations ought to be able to decide where supreme responsibility and command rests before the expedition starts, and not leave it for later haphazard arrangements by the commanders concerned, in much more difficult conditions, as laid down in Sec. 9 (3).

It is thought that the question of command is one on which the Chief of the Staff's sub-committee of the C.I.D.—or whatever takes its place in war—might well make a recommendation when submitting their joint appreciation to the Government (ibid Section 14 (4)).

PART II.—STRATEGY AND TACTICS

The danger of employing inadequate forces in the first instance

1. It is a common failing in British strategy to employ inadequate forces in the first instance. Sometimes it has been due to the special facilities available to an amphibious power for making the opening move, with the theoretical alternative

of an easy withdrawal if things go wrong. The complications involved in organizing the base establishment of a modern army render such withdrawal far more difficult than in the past as instance the Dardenelles, operations and the expeditions to North and South Russia. On other occasions the weakness of the forces used has been due to the inadequacy of the military resources at the disposal of the Government, a danger which seems likely to increase in inverse ratio to the size of our army. Occasionally the fault has lain in underestimating the resources of the enemy, as in the Dardenelles, or in a reluctance to deal too roughly with the enemy. Whatever the reason, the result has been that forces, insufficient to obtain a decision, have become detachments which failed to fulfil their proper function of containing superior forces of the enemy. Owing to indecision as to where lay the decisive point at the moment (Vol. I, p. 302), we were always short in Gallipoli of just that small extra margin of superiority necessary to success.

Our recent operations in China are noteworthy for not repeating the usual mistake.

Surprise

2. The absence of the element of surprise has already been mentioned. Stated as a demonstration to attract Turkish attention and relieve pressure on the Russians in the Caucasus, the measures taken by the Navy against the Dardenelles proved only too effective (Vol. I, pp. 109, 110).

Judged by modern standards the Turkish communications were poor, and had the attack secured even a moderate degree of strategic surprise, it could hardly have failed to succeed. But the months of warning given to the defence proved fatal to the enterprise.

Modern conditions are tending to increase the resisting power of small detachments, whilst improvements in communications enable the defence to appreciate and to rectify initial errors in distribution more rapidly than in the past. In consequence the element of surprise appears to be more important to the attacker than it has ever been. It might well advance from third to first place in the " Principles of War ".

Limitations of manœuvre areas and other conditions tend to increase the difficulty of giving this factor sufficient prominence in peace time manœuvres and exercises, with the result that there is a possible danger of failing to appreciate its supreme importance in war.

The superiority of the gun ashore over the gun afloat

3. This fact was borne out at Gallipoli as on the Belgian coast and at Scarborough. (It has recently received further

proof from the unexpected resistance of the Woosung forts to the Japanese bombardments.)

It is mentioned as being a justification of the new organization of coast defences at home, and as having a bearing on the size of the guns required at our overseas bases.

The war did not last long enough for seaborne attack from the air to be developed, but in the future it is likely to have greater chances of success.

One reservation must, however, be made that just as no artillery bombardment by itself will entirely destroy the resistance of good troops, neither will air attack.

The question or exercising command in modern conditions

4. Although in the light of after events it is possible to find fault with details of the plan for the initial landing on the Gallipoli Peninsula, generally speaking surprise was obtained and the plan was sound within the limited resources available.

That it broke down or failed to fulfil expectations was due to a variety of causes not all of which were avoidable.

The fact that the troops were landed away from the selected point ruined the Anzac operations from the start, converting them into a struggle against nature as much as against the Turks.

Everywhere, and particularly in the landings near the toe of the Peninsula, one of the great difficulties was to find out what was actually happening at the various beaches.

The same cause—bad communications rendered extremely difficult the exercise of command over the scattered troops of the 29th Division (Vol. I, p. 251). Both difficulties would have been greatly lessened had there been adequate air co-operation. Actually this was almost non-existent (Vol. I, p. 139).

The difficulty of control had been foreseen, with the result that the plan was too rigid, and looked too far ahead, providing for the continuance of operations in assumed conditions which did not actually eventuate. For whereas the two flank landing parties at " Y " and " S " beaches were practically unopposed, no advantage was gained, as they had been told to wait until the troops from the main beaches had advanced up to their level. (Vol. I, pp. 203, 237, 251.)

The main landings were seriously delayed, however, and received no held from the flank detachments, whose action would in all probability have cleared the front very rapidly had they been boldly handled.

Moreover, the reserves were put in where the attack was hung up, and persisted in attacking the stronger part of the enemy's defences, thus wasting time which could never be recaptured.

The last mistake was partly due to the commander of the 29th Division becoming engrossed in the landing taking place under his own eye, with a consequent loss of general perspective. (Vol. I, pp. 211, 213.)

The C.-in-C. who saw the opportunity presented by the success at " Y " beach, did not like to divert thither a portion of the reserves, which had all been handed over before the operations commenced to the 29th Division commander.

The conditions in the initial landing operations, as at Suvla Bay later, were admittedly unusual, but none the less they illustrate the difficulties which face the commander of a modern army deployed over a wide frontage and in considerable depth, *viz.*, to what extent he can maintain continuous control of operations as they develop.

The C.-in-C. is criticised for having retained no reserve under his own hand during the Helles and Anzac operations (Vol. I, p. 204), and similar criticism is directed against the Corps Commander at the Suvla Bay landing (Vol. II, p. 296).

On the other hand, the C.-in-C. was removed from his command after Loos, ostensibly because he had endeavoured to retain some power of influencing operations by keeping back a general reserve, instead of handing over everything to the Army Commander concerned. These instances illustrate the dilemma.

Broadly speaking, the three alternatives open to a commander are : —

(*a*) To retain control by retention of reserves.

(*b*) Like the G.O.C., 29th Division, to issue orders looking dangerously far ahead.

(*c*) To trust to the initiative of subordinate commanders and accept General Lee's solution—" My interference in battle would do more harm than good. I have then to rely on my brigade and divisional commanders. I think and work with all my power to bring the troops to the right place at the right time. Then I have done my duty. As soon as I order them forward into battle I leave my duty in the hands of God ".*

Rigid plans (alternative (*b*)) can be at once eliminated as highly undesirable, and it is the first (*a*) at which we should aim.

But it requires an improvement in communications both for the receipt of information as to the situation and the issue of orders.

---

* R.E. LEE by Sir F. Maurice, p. 142.

Improvements in reliability of aircraft ought to tend towards easing the difficulties of exercising command. We have recently had an example on a small scale in Kashmir of the kind of help to command which can be given by the R.A.F., acting as an aerial signal service*.

An alternative is the further development of ground signal communications. These already absorb an undesirable proportion of fighting strength, and simplification rather than elaboration is necessary. Wireless may help, but there are difficulties to be overcome.

Yet another solution is to increase the personal mobility of commanders by the provision of command armoured fighting vehicles; this has the great merit of simplicity and is worthy of consideration.

The development of initiative in subordinate commanders (F.S.R. II, 5, (4)) is of course most necessary, but there comes a point higher up where reliance on it may be dangerous, if accepted as a substitute for command.

The last and most attractive conception is to simplify the organization of battle by closing the weapons producing the supporting fire up to the troops supported, or better still to combine them in the same weapons.

If we could re-introduce the power to penetrate a weak front quickly, attack and defence would both tend to concentrate, and command would be correspondingly simplified by the shortening of communications in the actual battle.

At present the armoured fighting vehicle appears to offer the only prospect of success in this direction.

The position of headquarters

Conditions at the Gallipoli landings were naturally different in detail from those in normal field operations, but the same kind of difficulties presented themselves as in France and elsewhere.

At Gallipoli, headquarters were usually kept afloat in the first stages for fear of getting out of touch with the Navy, undoubtedly a solid reason.

As a result, perhaps, divisional headquarters ashore, both at Helles and Suvla, were greatly overloaded, whilst at Suvla brigade headquarters remained near the seashore. After the successful attacks on Chocolate and Green Hills on the evening of the 7th August by units of three brigades, the brigadiers concerned remained two miles in rear and great confusion resulted. No patrols were sent out and touch was lost with the enemy (Vol. II, p. 259).

* Rusi Journal, August, 1932, p. 489, *et seq.*

At Helles, on the other hand, most of the brigade and battalion commanders became casualties in the front line (Vol. I, pp. 228, 249, 251).

The matter is not easy.

F.S.R. II, 28 states that:—

"A commander should usually establish his headquarters sufficiently far in rear, so as to be beyond the reach of distractions by local events, but not so far distant that he cannot have quick personal access to his immediate subordinate commanders."

In modern conditions this means the provision of motor, and preferably armoured motor, transport down to infantry brigade commanders.

Responsibility for maintaining communication

6. A cognate question is dealt with in F.S.R. II, Sec. 28, and again in Chapter VIII. In this latter (Sec. 139, iv and v) the responsibility is laid on the junior for maintaining communication with his superior. He is thus tied to the rear instead of being free to follow his troops, just as in France he was held back by political anxiety for news. What, if any, are the arguments against reversing the responsibility, leaving the commander who is fighting free to concentrate on his forward communications for the purposes of command?

If the superior commander wants more information he can always in the last resort go forward and get it, whereas the reverse is not possible.

One might perhaps add that, as in the case of the artillery and troops supported (Sec. 28, 3) this should not absolve the junior commander from doing everything he can to assist in the maintenance of communication, but there is a big psychological difference between " assisting " and " being responsible ".

Superiority of the defence due to automatic weapons

7. Little can be learned from the three battles of Krithia following the landing operations, which was not equally brought out by the earlier experiences of attacks on the Western front, chief of which was the overwhelming superiority of the defence in modern conditions where attacked frontally.

Two Turkish battalions with four machine guns held up the whole of the 29th Division until Turkish reinforcements could be brought up (Vol. I, p. 364 note), and subsequent attacks merely exemplified what is well stated on page 350 of the official account, Vol. I.

" An advance by daylight, without adequate artillery support against unlocated machine gun positions is in nine cases out of ten a sheer impossibility."

It is fair to say that, with a few minor exceptions where heavy concentrations of artillery were achieved locally, no attacks, British or Turkish, whether by day or night, other than immediate counter-attacks, ever succeeded throughout the operations; this was due entirely to the inadequacy of artillery support. This is not surprising seeing that the available artillery was less than one-third of even the pre-war proportion (Vol. II, p. 58). Naval gun fire, once its moral effect had worn off, though overwhelming on paper, soon ceased to have much effect on the Turks, and in the later stages the presence of German submarines still further reduced its possibilities.

Value of advanced detachments in defence

8. A difficulty often overlooked in peace training, where the element of surprise in defence is usually absent, was in locating the exact positions of the enemy.

During the first two battles of Krithia concealed advanced detachments broke up the attack before contact was made with the enemy's main position (Vol. I, pp. 334, 336, 346). It is true that air reconnaissance was almost non-existent, but it is within the personal experience of most officers that similar posts in shelled areas on the Western front greatly added to the difficulties of staging an attack.

It is a means of maintaining for the defence the element of surprise, which is just as important as in attack. Further, as at Krithia, it usually forces on the attacker a number of preliminary operations which give time for the organization of the defence. I.T., Vol. II, 19 (3) stresses the point adequately.

Tendency to over-estimate the importance of high ground, to the detriment of " surprise " in defence

9. Possibly as a result of much training in mountain warfare against tribesmen, where to get above the enemy is to win the battle and to picket the heights is essential to safe communications, we are apt to beat our troops to pieces against the highest part of the enemy's position.

Such action may be thought to have the official sanction, for in F.S.R. II, 62 (4) we find:—

" if certain tactical localities or features can be captured, the action of the enemy will be seriously prejudiced. Such positions are likely to be the most strongly defended, and it is against them that the commander must develop his maximum fire power."

E

This action is frequently interpreted in peace exercises of all natures somewhat as follows: —

Search is made on the map for the highest parts of the enemy's position which then becomes the tactical feature of the greatest importance, a contention which it may not be easy to refute. It thus becomes the focus of the attack. The defender, for his part, unconsciously co-operates by selecting the highest points in the neighbourhood, including that chosen by the attack, as " points vital to the defence ", and the resulting battle is therefore staged in conditions which eliminate the element of surprise.

It is suggested that insufficient weight is given to the change created by air observation; that the importance of ground observation, which we learnt to appreciate so much in trench warfare from seldom having it, may be overstressed in mobile warfare.

In March 1918, the Germans moving up the valleys isolated the commanding positions and passed on, favoured it is true by fog. The protected resistance of the defenders of these positions delayed the attacker in places, but not nearly to the same general extent as if they had been directly attacked as we did in Gallipoli and elsewhere, and any further advance held up until they had been captured. It was this plan which the 29th Division adopted at Helles, hammering away at redoubts instead of pushing on past them, until the golden opportunity had passed away.

In the defence it is the machine guns rather than the artillery which are the great obstacle to the attacker. They do not require commanding ground for observation. On the contrary their hope of survival lies in concealment from view. For the artillery in the war air observation was found of greater value than ground observation, a fact of which we seem to be losing sight. Hills no longer conceal anything behind them as they did in the days when Wellington made his famous remark. They merely help the expert attacker, as bunkers on a golf course help the good player, by defining the objective. It may be argued that in peace exercises, with or without troops, the selection of a defensive position in level or nearly level country would make the running of the attack extremely difficult for everyone, including the directing staff. That is true, and if so it reinforces the value of this form of defensive position, which combines the two vital elements of surprise and concealment, with little real sacrifice of observation, given effective air co-operation. The fact of the matter is that to introduce information from the air on a realistic scale into peace exercises, particularly T.E.W.Ts., adds very greatly to the work of the directing staff, and is extremely difficult. In consequence we fall back on ground observation, which thus maintains a fictitious value from the point of view of war. Possibly we do not demand enough help—apart from actual flying—from the R.A.F. in the preparation of peace exercises.

It must be added that the foregoing remarks about defensive positions apply to positions hastily taken up for temporary occupation in mobile warfare. The advantages of the class of defensive position, indicated in F.S.R. II, 78, as selected by the Germans, for permanent occupations, are not open to argument; strength—natural and artificial—comfort, sanitation, reduction of demands on the R.A.F., etc., were all secured. The Turkish commanding positions on the Peninsula served them equally well.

The lesson is that neither in defence nor in attack should methods be stereotyped—each case should be judged according to circumstances. Comparatively level ground, possibly aided by a natural obstacle, may be a far stronger position than a range of hills. F.S.R. II, 78 under-states this principle. I.T. II, 19 and 20 put the case better. Our peace training is apt to lose sight of it.

Importance of creating salients in the attack

10. In the same order of ideas is a tendency in the attack for troops which are getting on to stop until those on the flanks come up into line with them, F.S.R. II, 64 (7) has it both ways.

Since the great object of the attacker is to create salients, as it is of the defender to avoid them, such situations are bound to occur as the first stage in any successful attack, and troops must be taught to welcome them as the first symptoms of success. This is not easy as troops dislike being shot into from a flank and, as is truly said in F.S.R. II, 65 (5), have a tendency to face towards the new danger.

The battles of Krithia, as well as the initial landings, provide several instances of troops stopping or falling back in such circumstances, but they had this excuse—that the vital importance of reinforcing success and not failure was but dimly recognized at that period in the army generally.

It is not necessary now to stress a point which has gone well home, but the difficulty of recognizing, in time, the point where success has been gained, and of acting on it, still remains.

Danger of giving alternative rôles to one body of troops

11. Out of the experiences of trench warfare, and in particular the German system of an elastic defence backed by a policy of carefully prepared immediate counterattack, came the great importance attached to consolidation.

It may have been necessary in the special circumstances, but it led to attacks being hampered by the men being overloaded with every kind of store, and consequently being very ready to stop. In mobile warfare there seems to be a real danger of giving a consolidation rôle to troops, if the primary necessity is, as it was at Suvla, to maintain an offensive attitude of mind. Consolidation is so safe and comfortable as compared with advancing into the unknown and away from the rations; apart from which, psychologically, troops cannot be expected to concentrate on more than one object at a time.

Very occasionally we may have suffered by going too far and too fast, but far more often unnecessary fear of counterattack, as at Helles and Suvla, paralyzed the advance, and valuable energy was wasted on "consolidation". F.S.R. II, 64 (11) and I.T. (Vol. II, 11 (31)), as expanded by Sec. 17, tend to foster what may develop into a grave fault. The disposition in depth of the machine guns and anti-tank weapons of the attack should in modern conditions of mobile warfare prove an adequate security against immediate counter-attack. F.S.R. II, 83 (6) supports this latter thesis.

Once troops start to dig in, the chances of getting them moving forward again are greatly reduced, and this is what happened at Suvla Bay:—

" ' You seem to be making yourselves snug ' said Sir M. Hankey who had gone ashore to see how the attack was progressing. ' We expect to be here for a long time ' was the reply."

Irresolution of command and the contributory causes

12. *The special lesson of the Suvla Bay landing* is the vital importance of taking full advantage of initial surprise in operations of this nature—of " going whilst the going is good ".

The lack of belief in the enterprise felt by the Commander and his B.G.G.S. was reflected throughout the force. It resulted in an absence of initiative, and readiness to relapse into a defensive rôle at the first sign of opposition, when offensive action was the one hope of success.

Attention is drawn in the official account (Vol. II, 150) to the misgivings of the B.G.G.S. which seem to have created the first doubts in the mind of his Corps Commander.

His objection to the plan as formulated by G.H.Q. was that " The whole teaching of the campaign in France proves that troops cannot be expected to attack an organized system of trenches without the assistance of a large number of guns. Consequently the capture of Chocolate and W. Hills could not be completed by dawn ". (Vol. II, 150.)

This is a good example of the danger of applying conclusions drawn from one set of operations to others entirely different. There was no organized system of trenches, and even had there been, the best chance, given the weakness of artillery, was to attack before dawn.

As Sir M. Hankey said (Vol. II, p. 277, note), " It looked as though this accursed trench warfare in France had sunk so deep into our military system that all idea of the offensive had been killed ".

PART III—ORGANIZATION AND EQUIPMENT

Artillery ammunition—shrapnel and high explosive

1. It was not sufficiently appreciated in the early stages of the Gallipoli campaign, nor for that matter in France or Palestine, that darkness, fog, or anything which reduces visibility is comparatively more advantageous to the attack than to the defence, if troops are well enough trained to profit by it. This is a powerful argument for smoke and gas shell, and also for H.E. as opposed to shrapnel, since in dry country, where we often fight, the effect of the high explosive shell in raising a dust cloud produces a screen not greatly inferior to smoke.

It is interesting to note that on the Peninsula the support of the French 75's, firing H.E., was far more effective than that of the British light artillery which fired only shrapnel. (Vol. II, pp. 48, 49, 92.)

Taking into consideration the complications involved in manufacturing shrapnel and in training troops—particularly those raised in war—to use it, the experiences of Gallipoli point to the advisability of relying entirely on H.E. and smoke shell, and abandoning shapnel. This step would reduce the difficulties now likely to be experienced in getting the right kind of ammunition up to the guns for any particular operation. Where so many other complications exist, any simplification is well worth some small sacrifice in other directions.

Before the Great War, apart from a few case shot, we carried only shrapnel. To it have now been added smoke, H.E., and perhaps assorted gas shell. It was possible to use these as circumstances required in practically static conditions, with an elaborate system of communications organized at leisure, but will it be so in mobile warfare?

The same principle applies to the artillery as to the infantry or cavalry, viz., that it cannot carry always everything it may only want occasionally, but only what is most generally useful.

Shrapnel is useless against any form of head cover and less effective against the trenches and armoured vehicles likely to be employed by a first-class enemy. Is it worth retaining for use against a second- or third-class enemy who may allow himself to be caught in the open?

Guns versus Howitzers

2. Linked to the question of shrapnel is that of the proportion of guns to howitzers. So long as shrapnel remained the main projectile, guns would naturally have the preference, but with its abolition the policy might need revision.

The present 18-pr. equipment was designed as a barrage gun, and if the firing of barrages is not feasible as the main method of support in mobile warfare, howitzers should be increased.

Moreover, it seems probable that the defence will go to ground on every possible occasion and the experiences of Gallipoli—as elsewhere—indicate the definite superiority of the howitzer against troops under cover.

The main arguments on the other side are:—

(a) The superiority of the gun against armoured fighting vehicles, and

(b) That troops can get closer up to their own covering fire when provided by guns as opposed to howitzers.

But against this latter must be put the greater facility for getting howitzers into positions near the front line, the absence of crest clearing problems and so forth, with all the corresponding advantages of shortened communications.

Weight carried by the infantry soldier

3. The well conceived operations from Anzac to turn the Turkish flank in connection with the Suvla Bay landing were hampered by a variety of causes inherent in night operations, over unreconnoitred and extremely difficult country—hesitation on the part of commanders, loss of direction, and so forth.

A powerful contributory cause was the heavy load carried by the troops, including as it did 200 rounds of ammunition, one day's rations per man, and heavy tools on the scale of one pick or shovel to every eight men. The troops were in any case unfit owing to a considerable period of trench fighting in hot weather and were called upon to engage in practically mountain warfare.

The enterprise failed mainly owing to the troops being beaten by fatigue long before they reached the summit of the hills (Vol. II, p. 196). This overloading of the infantry soldier was a common occurrence in Gallipoli—as on the Western front —the idea being that having reached the objective he should be self supporting until rearward services of some kind could be organized.

It resulted usually in the men failing to carry out the first stage of the programme, *viz.*, reaching their objectives, or in their throwing away most of their impediments, which led to the very shortage of ammunition, etc., which it was desired to avoid. (Vol. I, pp. 197, 291.)

If our infantry is to be " capable of operating over almost any ground either by day or night " (F.S.R. II, 10 (2) which is its chief, if not its sole remaining asset, its equipment must be lightened. We cannot expect it to achieve the impossible. As one battalion commander said of the Anzac turning movement in August—"Our physical condition was very poor, and we had heavy loads to carry. I doubt if they could have marched the distance required in the time, given daylight, proper guides and no opposition ". (Vol. II, p. 192.)

Of two evils it seems better to run a chance of not being able to hold the objective when reached, than to make a certainty of never reaching it.

It is of course objectionable to increase transport by carrying a part of the infantryman's kit, but we have taken weight off the horse to make cavalry more mobile and the same arguments appear to apply at least as much to infantry.

The alternative, *viz.*, to carry the man as well as his kit, would be more costly and cumbersome, and can only be applied to a small portion of an army.

Special equipment required in the case of opposed landings

4. The difficulties of making a landing in the face of opposition, serious enough in the days of Gallipoli, have since been increased by the additional number of automatic weapons forming the normal equipment of even second-class armies.

As on land, the necessity for the provision of armoured vehicles is indicated, and was met at Suvla by using armoured motor lighters (Vol. II, p. 131) specially built by the Admiralty for Lord Fisher's Baltic scheme.

Had these lighters carried tanks, or had there been amphibian tanks available, the success of the operations would probably have been ensured from the start.

This provides a useful example of going to modern scientific developments for the antidote to difficulties created by science, and the importance of constantly studying in peace time how scientific developments may effect military means and methods.

Proportion of peace effectives to war establishments

5. The three divisions engaged in the Suvla landing belonged to the K.I. army, were composed for the most part of the flower of the country's manhood, had been training for 10 months and contained a large proportion of regular officers and N.C.Os. (Vol. II, p. 139.)

Yet we find the 29th Division after being repeatedly shot to pieces considered to be a more efficient instrument up to the end.

We all had our different experiences, and may draw different conclusions. My own service was mainly with a regular division (4th) and rightly or wrongly, we held the conviction that—like the 29th Division—we could sustain losses and absorb new material with less loss of efficiency than could divisions comprising units without the same traditions.

This is only mentioned because it may have a bearing on a point which must be exercising many minds at the present time, *viz.*, do we get better value from maintaining in peace time a larger number of units so weak that training is difficult, or should we do better to have a smaller number at a higher peace establishment and consequently better trained and more easily mobilized.

The answer really depends on what is the most important purpose for which the British Army is maintained, and what is the best form of Army for that purpose. This raised questions of wide extent and great magnitude, but for the purposes of this discussion they can be narrowed down to two major alternatives : —

(i) The first is to maintain in peace time a regular army in a high standard of readiness with the idea that the promptness of its intervention may enable it to meet the needs of the Empire without serious expansion.

(ii) The second alternative is to recognize that the regular army can only gain time for the development of far stronger forces after the outbreak of war. What the nature of the forces may be does not affect this broad aspect of the question.

Past history, the present world wide commitments of the British Empire, and the time required to organize sea transport for the move of any considerable force to some of the likely storm centres, all indicate that the second is more probably the correct answer, as stated in F.S.R., Vol. II, p. 3 (3).

Apart from the maintenance of obligatory garrisons overseas, the importance of the army lies not so much in what it is in peace, as into what it will expand in war. If this is accepted— as I think it must be—then the experiences of the past indicate that the important factor is the efficiency of the cadres of officers and N.C.Os., on which the new units and formations will be built, and not the standard of training of those individual private soldiers who can never rise to anything more. The latter can be produced comparatively quickly when the time comes.

That being the case we are probably right in continuing to accept the difficulties of training at home with weak effectives, and the expense of what might appear to be too high a proportion of officers and N.C.Os., as being the lesser evil.

To what extent the peace time training of the Territorial Army will be found to supply something of the necessary fibre in war remains to be seen. It is, however, safe to assume that it must be a better system of expansion than that adopted in 1914, when apparently the value of the framework which already existed in the Territorial Force was insufficiently appreciated, and the raising of the New Army was initiated de novo.

The closer association of the Territorial Army with the Regular Army appears to be a move in the right direction, as tending to increase the powers of expansion of the latter by improving the efficiency of the former.

The necessity for variety in peace training

6. In connection with the Suvla Bay operations attention has been drawn to the application of lessons from trench warfare conditions in France to open warfare conditions in Gallipoli, with disastrous results to the latter.

The British Army has to fight under such varied conditions that officers must be trained to judge a military problem purely on its own merits, and not be permitted to base themselves on general rules applicable to all conditions, which rules cannot in fact be formulated.

We are too fond of quoting some dictum by higher authority, pronounced possibly in quite different set of circumstances.

This means that we should be given, in peace time, as much variety of experience as possible, and such variety of experience is provided by the difference in conditions at the various stations at home and abroad, if advantage is taken of local facilities.

Our training has perhaps been too stereotyped; apt to neglect local conditions and consequently to fail in developing common sense.

Value of peace training

7. A side light on the relations between peace and war training is that an officer who on two occasions during the Suvla operations did nothing when action. was imperatively necessary, acted in exactly the same way 16 years later in similar circumstances in peace manœuvres.

Presumably, like many others during the war, he had found it safer to play for safety than to risk censure by doing something which might be wrong.

The lesson is of course that every form of initiative should be encouraged in peace training, so that the habit of taking positive as opposed to negative decisions may be acquired by all officers at an early stage in their careers.

As regards T.E.W.Ts., a clear distinction should be drawn between those designed to practise the machinery of command, organization of covering fire, or some such special aspect of the " drill " of battle, and those designed to develop the initiative and powers of decision of commanders. Both are necessary, but until 1932 we have perhaps had rather too many of the former. Further there is a tendency, not confined to this country, for high commanders to get down to too much detail in the handling of small bodies of troops.

For exercises to develop powers of reasoning and decision the intelligence side must be developed, and the fog of war introduced. Have we progressed since the war in this respect? The idea has been, doubtless, that we should " learn to walk before trying to run ", but this can be overdone.

Promotion by selection as opposed to seniority

8. Another lesson which may be indicated is the danger of sticking too rigidly to seniority for command in the field. As Lord Kitchener said when he finally removed some of the senior commanders from Gallipoli: " This is a young man's war, and we must have C.Os. who will take full advantage of opportunities which occur but seldom ".

A self-confident junior may be more ready to make a decision on his own responsibility than one of greater experience, who may be lacking in powers of decision, or physical fitness, or both, as was the case at Suvla. Stamina is particularly important in campaigns in Eastern theatres, where the physical strain is greater than in temperate climates.

The most able and experienced officers abroad are sometimes tired, whilst those at home may be lacking in experience and habit of command. If the British Army is likely to have to fight seriously in an Eastern theatre, it seems important in peace time to give experience of conditions there to all officers likely to rise to high rank.

Peace training of infantry

9. The number of routine duties which fall on the infantry in peace time, the low strength of home battalions, the growing complexity of training and the number of specialists required, create difficulties of which we are all aware.

Leaving on one side the question of a possible simplification in training by a reduction in the number of weapons carried, it is for consideration whether, as matters stand, we make the best use of the time available.

Conditions vary in different stations at home and abroad, and everywhere training is hampered by some factor; crops, climate, weak effectives, moves to the hills, leave and so forth, as the case may be.

But in every case there is one factor in common, viz., that the year never seems to be long enough to include all the training which should be done to produce a really efficient, up-to-date soldier.

So far as the army at home is concerned, a common limiting factor, becoming more and more serious as we go North into a longer winter and shorter summer, is the absolute priority of reasonable weather given to shooting on the range over all other forms of training. Is this good value?

A big game hunter takes all reasonable provision to enable him to hit the quarry when he has made his stalk, but that is a minor difficulty as compared with reaching the desired position from which to take the shot. This latter requires far higher intelligence and training. The tactics in which alone good rifle shooting will help the infantryman forward, *viz.*, infiltration, skilful leadership, correct judging of distance, and use of ground, are akin to stalking, and are equally more difficult than the actual shooting.

It is not contested that amongst the first duties of the infantryman is the ability to shoot straight and have confidence in his weapons, if only as an aid to morale; but I suggest that we go beyond that at present.

In speeches after rifle meetings we are fond of recalling that the rapid fire of the British infantry was barely distinguishable from that of machine guns (by which, as a matter of fact, it would now probably be replaced). But we lose sight of the fact that a large proportion of the infantry in question were reservists with strange rifles, who had not fired even a refresher course for a year or more. As a fact since the earliest times our shooting has been good, because shooting in battle is a matter of temperament and the British soldier does not get excited, as do so many others who shoot equally well on the ranges but fail in war.

Surely the conclusion is that once the soldier has been well grounded, it is not absolutely necessary for him to fire any considerable number of rounds annually, and that here we may prove a step further towards the ideal of progressive training over a cycle of years.

It is true that this will not help the units at home so much as those overseas, owing to the large proportion of first year men who must be well grounded; but if we regard shooting on the range as being a means to an end and not, as at present, an end in itself, we should be far more elastic as regards both the number of rounds fired and their interference with other training.

Unless some saving is made in this direction it is difficult to see how we can find time to improve the general training of infantry and increase the potential supply of N.C.Os. in war.

At present, whatever may be the intentions of the Army Council in the matter, accuracy on the range has a connection with pay, whilst every battalion, if not competing with others in the matter of average, is trying to beat its last year's figures. This may be contested; but I would point out that at Hythe a special demonstration is, or was, given to the senior officers' course, of how to prevent cheating in the annual weapon training course—which shows that the average soldier thinks about it.

So long as this state of affairs exists, commanders, in fairness to the men, will try to equalize weather conditions at the expense of the collective training period.

Let us get back to the real object of shooting on the range, viz., the development of confidence in his weapons in the average soldier, leaving higher shooting to the rifle meetings, which have a useful function in maintaining the attainable standard.

The necessity for developing the offensive spirit in peace training

10. But however ably we may allot the time available for training, it is to be feared that it will never be entirely adequate to cover all operations and aspects of war equally comprehensively. To a certain extent we must specialize.

Given the devastating effect of modern arms, it is certain that trenches will be employed whenever it is possible to do so. Trench warfare is comparatively easy, however, and bullets will teach men to go to ground soon enough.

In peace training we should to avoid a trench mentality, and to inculcate what is infinitely more difficult, *viz.*, the determination to push on when every natural instinct points to staying under cover.

In defence the British soldier has never failed to acquit himself admirably, and defence is much easier than it used to be. The most difficult operation of war now seems to be to attack, and to keep the attack going after the carefully prepared initial stage has passed.

As we found on many occasions, a hole can be plugged very quickly with machine guns, in comparison with the time required to get infantry forward against them under organized covering fire; and with mechanization machine guns can now move more quickly than during the war.

Taking these facts into consideration, one is forced to recognize that the soldier moving on his feet is too slow for the purposes of reserve in attack, if we are to seize fleeting opportunities for the development of initial success.

Our peace training in the attack breaks down owing to the inadequacy of the means available. For the initial attack more covering fire is necessary, for the subsequent stages a commander requires an instrument sharper and more mobile than infantry on foot.

The same remarks apply to any counter-attack, or indeed to any form of offensive.

Lacking the means to attack successfully, it is a strong temptation to trainers of troops to give priority to the defensive.

Conclusion

11. The outstanding lesson of the Gallipoli campaign is the decisive increase in the power of the defence due to automatic weapons.

No longer can training and discipline alone overcome the resistance of second or even third class troops, as the Japanese have found to their cost in the operations round Chapei.

These latter reinforce the lessons of the war, and must be a warning to us, who are required to control enormous numbers and areas with a diminishing quota of troops increasingly handicapped by international conventions. The statesmen of the day appear to under-estimate the effect on our ability to face up to our military responsibilities, should those who have no such problems succeed in removing the last remaining asset of the civilized forces, *viz.*, the products of science as applied to the problems of war.

Policy also tends to increase the number of automatic weapons in the hands of troops of non-British origin. A police army, like a police force, cannot act defensively, but must take the offensive promptly against incursion or insurrection.

The whole problem of war, as affecting the British Army, is how to restore the lost superiority of the offensive, and more particularly the relative superiority of a small well equipped army against second or third class enemies, whose numbers are unlimited, whose administrative wants remain simple, but whose armament continues to improve.

Our efforts to restore striking power by concentrated support of artillery have hitherto led to delays in launching an attack, which delays may, as in Gallipoli, frequently prove of even greater value to the enemy.

If we are to rely mainly on artillery support, then the plan of attack must be dominated by the requirements of the artillery. Our manuals hardly make this point strongly enough (F.S.R. II, 61 (3), 65 (1) (ii)). Infantry Training Vol. II misses the point entirely. By this means some of the present delays in organizing artillery support may be reduced.

But the difficulties inherent in the problem will remain, because no means is in sight for eliminating the complications involved in connecting shell and target. Still more so must this be the case with covering machine gun fire, because it may often be impossible to tell when connection has been established, owing to inability to locate the strike of the bullets.

Increase in static machine guns is no answer to the problem, in fact they might well prove to be an encumbrance, as reducing the mobility of the infantry in which they are at present incorporated. This is an argument for the creation on mobilization of heavy machine gun units, to be used for holding as opposed to attacking rôles.

A modern army has become like a muscle-bound boxer; able to stand a good deal of punishment, and to deliver a weighty punch if the opponent will stay quite still whilst it is coming.

This may meet the needs of the French on a heavily fortified frontier, but is not at all the kind of army required by the circumstances of the British Empire.

The only alternative appears to be a greater reliance on armoured fighting vehicles. It is no exaggeration to say that a battalion, or even a company of tanks at Suvla and possibly Krithia would have ensured a rapid and complete success.

They alone at the present time appear to be capable of restoring that power to deliver a quick and powerful blow, which was lost by armies of yesterday.

(Sgd.) W. KIRKE,
Lt.-General.

September, 1932.

APPENDIX IV

REPORT ON OPERATIONS IN EGYPT AND PALESTINE UP TO JUNE, 1917, BY COLONEL (TEMPORARY BRIGADIER) A. J. McCULLOCH, D.S.O., D.C.M., A.D.C.

References, except where otherwise stated, are to—The History of the Great War—Military Operations—Egypt and Palestine, Vol. I.

LESSON I.—THE DEFENDER SHOULD TAKE ADVANTAGE OF NATURAL OBSTACLES IN ORDER TO STOP THE ATTACKER

" The Defence of the Suez Canal "

In this case the obstacle was the comparatively waterless Peninsula of Sinai, traversed by three indifferent routes. These constituted defiles through the obstacle.

Throughout the war our commanders proposed three distinct and different plans for the defence of the Canal.

The Official History of Australia in the War of 1914-18 (Vol. VII, p. 43) states:—

> " The crossing of this desert land has been deemed a difficult Military undertaking only because the wide intervals between oases necessitated a swift and uninterrupted passage. But rapid progress was generally made easy by the fact that the defenders awaited attack in the well-watered region on their side of the wilderness. The invader was always allowed to pass the desert; the decisive battles were fought either on the fringe of Egypt or on the fertile slopes of Southern Palestine."

There is a certain amount of confusion of mind among officers as to the ways of using the advantage which an obstacle, with few defiles, confers on the defender.

As proof of this compare the 1915 plan of Defence.

Posts to safeguard the Canal were located not on the enemy's side, but on the Western side of the Canal. This plan was criticised in that the Canal seemed to be defending the troops—not the troops defending the Canal.

It is suggested that the methods of utilizing the obstacle are of two kinds:—

(1) The defender may use a comparatively large number of troops defending the actual defiles, and he will reinforce these troops when it is ascertained which defile the enemy is using.

The defender will usually employ this course when he is not yet strong enough to assume the offensive, but wishes to delay a decision and stop the enemy. (C/f. Romani, 4th August, 1916.)

(2) He may use proportionately few troops to remain on the defiles, merely watching to see which the enemy selects, but not actually defending the defiles.

The defender will keep his main force on his side of the obstacle in a central position. Then he will strike the attacker while the latter is in difficulties passing the defile, or while the attacker has part of his force through, and part of his force not through the defile, and not deployed.

This method will usually be employed if the defender wishes to resume the offensive by counter-stroke.

One of the strategical problems which again may confront Britain in the future is the utilization of the Sinai Desert for defence of the Suez Canal.

If a great land Power based on Russia and the Middle East is at War with a great sea Power, she will seek vulnerable points in that sea Power's L. of C. One of the few points at which she can strike is the Suez Canal.

Will Britain, to defend the Suez Canal, keep her forces:—

(1) In Palestine, holding Beersheba—Gaza, or some other line?
(2) El Auja and El Arish? (the 2nd plan of 1916).
(3) The line used in July, 1916, including Romani (the 1st plan of 1916).

Many considerations will have to be taken into account, and the actual case would have to be presented to get at the right solution. Various solutions were produced during the War. They cannot all have been correct.

However, as regards the theoretical problem of the utilization of any obstacle for defence, this is a matter which merits some thinking and stating. I suggest the proper use of a natural obstacle by the defender might form a profitable study in a Command or other Exercise.

LESSON 2.—FEINT OR HOLDING ATTACKS MUST NOT BE HALF-HEARTED ATTACKS, OR THEY WILL IMPOSE ON NO ONE

Turkish attack on Suez Canal—3rd February, 1915

The Turks attacked Tussum, and feinted against El Kubri, El Ferdan and Kantara. (Vol. I, p. 46.)

These feint attacks were all conducted with so little resolution, as to fail completely in their object. Contrast our feint attack at 3rd Battle of Gaza. Here the Turk was fixed by our 21st Corps, so that his attention was not drawn to the real attack *via* Beersheba.

It is suggested that a Commander should tell only his Chief Staff Officer, and as few others as possible, that an attack is meant to be a feint or holding attack. How then will he convey his intentions to all his Subordinates? Those he will instruct that an attack (not meant to be pushed to its limit, and meant only to divert attention) is to be carried as far as an objective which will not involve undue loss.

But the Chief Commander must shoulder the responsibility of saying how far this attack is to go. He must *not* leave this decision to his Subordinates. Otherwise the bold may go too far, and the cautious not far enough. Furthermore, no one wishes to be killed in a feint attack.

LESSON 3.—WHEN A COMMANDER OF A FORCE IN A POSITION OF DEFENCE SENDS A DETACHED FORCE OUT FROM THAT POSITION, ITS MISSION AND ACTION IN CASE OF ATTACK MUST BE CLEARLY DEFINED

Many unfortunate incidents in the Great War arose from subordinates not being clear as to their rôle.

Action of the 5th Mounted Brigade, Katia—23rd April, 1916

Two Squadrons Worcester Yeomanry, and later one Squadron Gloucester Yeomanry held their position, fought it out and were wiped out. Of the remainder, some withdrew without fighting, others withdrew fighting. It was not, however, the intention of the Commander to make a serious resistance to the Turkish attack, and in such circumstances the Brigadier's orders were to retire on Dueiden, or Railhead. Subordinate Commanders, however, did not carry out this rôle.

The question is one which arises whenever outposts are employed in front of a defensive position.

As laid down in F.S.R. II, outposts may be used for three objects:—

(1) To deceive the enemy.
(2) To protect the Main Body.
(3) To warn the Main Body.

They may be handled in three ways:—

(1) Resist to the last man and round. This is easy but painful. A Commander may not wish to see part of his force killed without fair return for his money.
(2) Withdraw fighting as does a rearguard—a difficult yet a recognized operation.
(3) Withdraw as soon as warning is given to the Main Force. This is easy, and usually painless.

F

During Training, orders are often vague on these points, *e.g.*, Serjt. " A " with No. 6 Platoon is sent out to point " X ". All he is told is that he is a detached post or an outpost.

I suggest that Inspecting Officers should pay more attention to finding out from Post Commanders themselves what their orders are.

LESSON 4.—THE MOBILITY OF A DETACHMENT IS THAT OF ITS LEAST MOBILE COMPONENT

The affair at Katia—23rd April, 1916

The presence of discounted Engineers at Oghratina, and of dismounted details at Katia led the Mounted Yeomanry to stay in order to extricate their comrades. Otherwise, the Yeomanry should, in accordance with their appointed rôle, have withdrawn to avoid disaster at the hands of an overwhelming force of Turks.

This fact needs bringing home to those engaged in Tactical Exercises without and with Troops.

For example, Infantry in Busses are sometimes included with an Armoured Force. This is often quite reasonable. The Armoured Force is a " seize, grab and bolt " agent, and cannot hold the place it has taken. Infantry can. But it must be borne in mind that Bussed Infantry tie the Armoured Force, or part of it, to roads.

For the same reason Cavalry are sometimes rightly attached to an Armoured Force. But it must be remembered that it is cramping the mobility of a 12 m.p.h. Force to include with it a 5 m.p.h. Force.

At Tactical Exercises with Troops one sometimes sees Field Artillery attached to a Cavalry Force. Reasons for this may justify it, but is it always remembered that the mobility of a 5 m.p.h. Force may be reduced by including with it a 3 m.p.h. Force?

LESSON 5.—THE VALUE OF SURPRISE

Lack or Surprise

Reference F.S.R., Vol. II, Sec. 8 (iii), and 63. 1 (iii) (2).

Of all the weapons in the armoury of the offensive (as compared with the defensive) surprise is the strongest.

Yet Kress von Kressentein attacked where he was expected.

" To Sir A. Murray it appeared that the enemy Commander was bound down to one plan of operations. It was incredible that he should throw his main weight against the prepared defences. *What was anticipated* was a containing attack against these defences and an attack with all available strength against the British right South of Katib Gannit. A manœuvre of this nature would obviously expose the Turkish left flank to an attack by mounted troops, an arm in which the British were strong and the enemy weak." (Vol. I, p. 103.)

One of the commonest errors committed by Commanders in the War was to attack where the enemy expected attack and was ready for it, and it is this fact more than any other which induced civilian opinion, as mirrored in post-War novels, to consider Military Commanders wasteful of life and unresourceful.

The 2nd Battle of Gaza may be cited as a further illustration. The value of surprise was not realized by the Force Commander when, prior to his attack:—

(1) He made reconnaissances in force at his point of attack, pp. 327-329.
(2) His attack was made in two stages, with a day intervening, p. 330.
(3) Between the two stages a bombardment took place, pp. 331, 334.

" A Commander who selects the offensive is able to select his point of attack. He is also more likely to surprise his opponent, and to be able to develop superior Forces at the decisive place." (F.S.R., Vol. II, Sec. 23 (2).) It might well be added " A Commander who selects the offensive, and fails to surprise his opponent has lost the main advantage which the offensive confers."

It seems that one of the shortcomings of our Regulations is that they do not sufficiently emphasize the factor of Surprise and Deception.

The value of Surprise and its neglect by Commanders in the War is only too apparent. How can we arrange in Peace Training that the coming Commanders will not make the same error?

The following solution is suggested:—

Few Exercises as set admit of any Surprise. They usually result in attacking or defending some position, and criticism is throttled down to dealing with " how he does it "— not " what does he do? "

To contrive opportunity for Surprise needs arrangement, but it is well worth it. I practised it when Commanding an Infantry Brigade and found that it lent zest to the Manœuvre and created interest. I used to ask Officers of all ranks which Manœuvre day they liked the best. They all selected the day when something unexpected was sprung on them.

Training and Manœuvre Regulations, p. 72, para. 8 says:—

" It is an essential of skilled Directorship to introduce Surprise."

How often is this done?

       F 2

If we want to get value from our Exercises, let Directors make a practice of introducing new factors to give scope for Surprise and Deception.

Some Exercises might be set, both with and without troops, which place in the Commander's hands a force which he can use as a weapon of Surprise.

Directors should try to praise ruse and cunning whenever they can, *e.g.*, laying out of a dummy H.Q. to mislead the enemy aircraft; keeping a Tank back to make a noise on the opposite flank to that selected for attack.

I suggest that Brigade and Divisional Commanders should be encouraged to introduce more imagination and scope for Surprise into their Exercises.

LESSON 6.—TO DELIVER THE COUNTER-STROKE AT THE PROPER PLACE AND TIME THE COMMANDER MUST BE IN CLOSE TOUCH WITH THE BATTLE. OF ALL MILITARY OPERATIONS A COUNTER-STROKE REQUIRES THE MOST DELICATE TIMING

At Romani the situation for preparing a counter-stroke was usually favourable:—

(1) We knew where the attack would come.
(2) We out-numbered the enemy.
(3) The enemy were bound to be tired owing to heat and want of water.

Yet the counter-stroke was:—

(1) Mis-timed.
(2) Not co-ordinated.

The Commander should have been near Romani, and not at Kantara 20 miles away.

The question arises, can a counter-stroke be managed with large forces and with the complications of modern warfare? Is the manœuvre only possible with small forces? The question seems to be mainly one of inter-communication.

The command post has to fulfil two requirements:—

(1) Touch with the situation.
(2) Ability to give the word " go " to Reserves.

It is no longer possible for a Commander to watch the course of the whole battle. It is very much more difficult to determine the exact time for the intervention of reserves, and to issue orders and get these reserves to the selected spot before the opportunity for success has passed.

The counter-attack and counter-offensive require constant and delicate timing.

The classification in F.S.R. Vol. II, into immediate and deliberate counter-attacks and the counter-offensives, is appropriate.

The chief causes of failure in the War were:—

(1) *Immediate Counter-attacks.*—The main cause of failure was want of reconnaissance, of plan, of preparation, of rehearsal.

The lesson can easily be taught, and should be taught more during Company and Battalion training, and is best taught at Operations involving small Forces.

Rarely would a Force of over a battalion be used in an Immediate Counter-Attack.

(2) *Deliberate Counter-attacks.*—During the War the main causes of failure was want of Command and Control.

To bring off a deliberate counter-attack a Commander must be in touch with:—

(*a*) The situation.
(*b*) His Reserve.

In Peace Training, however, the Commander has no shells nor bullets to think about, is not prone to keep away from the battle and is usually ready to throw his weight about.

At Training in the Field, Directors should ensure that Commanders hold the happy mean between being so far back that they are not in touch, and being so far forward that they would be too easily knocked out by hostile fire.

(3) *The Counter-offensive.*—The War has shown that with large forces the premeditated counter-offensive as at Austerlitz is difficult to manage.

When one considers the counter-offensives in the Great War, one cannot give the Commanders credit for appreciating " Reculer pour mieux sauter " or of preparing a trap as the Pratzen Heights proved to the Russians at Austerlitz.

Yet the employment of means to entrap, mislead and deceive the enemy might well be more studied by young Officers. Some of them will be Commanders of our Armies one day, and the talents which go to the " make up " of a General should be early kept in view. Army Training Memorandum 4. A. of 1932, should have the desired effect.

The strong determined ruthless Commander is to-day apt to be a nuisance. What we want is a skilful, versatile, imaginative Leader, able to take advantage of the machines the XXth Century has put in his hand, full of ruse, yet bold enough to take risks.

LESSON 7.—UNLESS INFANTRY ARE FIT FOR MARCHING THE FRUITS OF VICTORY ARE APT TO BE MISSED. (SEE VOL. I, p. 201)

The C.-in-C., M.E.F., wrote:—

" I cannot pursue · with all the vigour I should like because my Infantry, and the Horses of the Mounted Division are exhausted . . . I am informed by G.O.C., 52nd Division, that many of his men are physically incapable of making a sustained effort ".

This was by no means an isolated case.

There is no use blinking at the fact that as Infantry soldiers our mens' physical fitness is defective. This seems to be inevitable in an over industralized nation.

To make up for physical defects inherent in a town-bred population we should see that one of the functions of our Peace Time Army is to be a School of Physical Training.

Closely connected with the subject of the soldier's mobility and endurance is that of the weight we ask him to carry.

Can we expect the same man to be a beast of burden and a fighter? No.

We have heard of the problem of how the attacking Infantry are to cross the last 500 yards.

The creeping barrage and the Tank were invented as keys to the solution. The defects are that the barrage wants too much ammunition, and the Tank is to vulnerable. How can we reduce these defects? A suggested solution is to increase the speed of the Infantry.

Take the case of a battalion with an objective 1,000 yards wide having to cross a dangerous zone of 1,000 yards. An ordinary estimate for the time in crossing is 20 minutes. About 40 guns and 2,400 rounds will be wanted to deal with the task.

Suppose the Infantry could move at 200 yards a minute, then only 5 minutes would be wanted. This would allow the task to be done with 600 rounds—a wonderful saving.

Take the Tank support case:—

To cover 1,000 yards, the Tanks will take some $2\frac{1}{2}$ minutes. If the Infantry take 20 minutes the Tanks will have to remain on the objective $17\frac{1}{2}$ minutes, otherwise enemy machine guns which have kept hidden will come to life and take toll of the attacker.

But if the Infantry take 5 minutes, the Tanks will only have to stay some $2\frac{1}{2}$ minutes. This should reduce their casualties enormously.

If the Infantry has to carry 56 lbs. as now (nearly half his own weight) we cannot expect him to do 200 yards a minute. But what if we aim at real mobility and reduce his load to 28 lbs.

The Pathan has taught us the lesson that the man with the rifle must be a mover.

If we cannot have all our Infantry going " into the ring " with proper fighting kit, let us revive Light Infantry. They may push forward to seize the fruit and the ordinary Infantry may follow and safeguard it.

It would be dangerous, however, to treat them as " Sturm truppen ".

LESSON 8.—THE DANGER OF UNNECESSARY TRANSFER OF CON-DUCT OF THE BATTLE TO SUBORDINATES, AND OF DIVIDED COMMANDS

1st Gaza—26th March, 1917

The C.-in-C. handed over the operation of invading Palestine, his main pre-occupation, to a subordinate commander.

The latter in turn handed over the main part of the Battle of Gaza, his main pre-occupation, to another subordinate commander. Yet he continued to mix himself up in the operation.

The C.-in-Cs. Headquarters at El Arish was in touch by telephone with Eastern Force Headquarters at In Seriat. This was at the side of the Headquarters which had been made responsible for the conduct of the Battle. (Vol. I, p. 288.) The Subordinate of two commanders almost inevitably feels himself cramped in his conduct of an action if his superior is on top of him.

The C.-in-C. was ostensibly superior in experience, and at handling troops, to either of the subordinate commanders concerned. Why, therefore, did he not concentrate his force of Generalship, as well as his force of troops, at the place where he called for a decision?

During the later phases of the occupation, the C.-in-C. himself shouldered the responsibility of managing operations. This gave better results.

LESSON 9.—FAILURE TO REINFORCE SUCCESS WHERE ACHIEVED

1st Battle of Gaza

Two Mounted Divisions, and one Division had surrounded Gaza when night fell on 26th March, defeating some seven Turk Battalions. One more Division, and one Brigade were at hand available.

Another Division (less a Brigade) was 10 miles off.

Reserves should have been pushed on to complete success, and consolidate gains. Yet, because of possible counter-attack by two enemy Divisions on the morning of 27th March, and another weak enemy Division by midday, 27th March, this was not done. Even the successful troops were withdrawn.

We failed to reinforce success where it had been won on this occasion. Again at the 2nd Battle of Gaza we pushed in more riflemen to try to retrieve failure.

The lesson has borne fruit and is recorded in F.S.R. II, Sec. 64 (8).

It was in Ludendorf's tactical injunctions issued prior to 21st March, 1918, that infiltration methods acquired prominence.

Ludendorf, following Sir John Moore, adopted the tactics of the stalker. By stealth the Infantry Section was to discover where the German shells had blown a sufficient hole for a soft spot to be created. It then exploited the soft spot. Reserves hurried to the spot. Infiltration followed.

We now know the value of this tactic. Have we emphasized it enough in our Manuals? Can we instil it more in practice?

It is suggested that F.S.R. II, Sec. 64. 13, requires elucidation; it states:—

> " If he is satisfied that these factors are in his favour, he must not hesitate to employ his reserves for this purpose, even if the enemy's resistance has hitherto been successful."

Now, if this is interpreted to mean " employ his Reserves " *of Infantrymen* are we correct? He may bring Tank, Artillery, machine gun Reserves up and so create an opportunity for Infantry, but if his only answer to successful enemy resistance is " more Infantry " the Commander is still thinking in old pre-War terms of attacking with flesh, and has not acquired the proper conception of an attack of flesh, plus shells and bullets.

We admit that Infantry may get along against unorganized defence with their own weapons, but they cannot succeed with such against organized defence with machine guns in position.

Against organized defence which has already held up Infantry, increased Infantry with the same fire support will not succeed, although the same may succeed with increased fire support. By teaching in the field the necessity of a " fire " plan in addition to a " movement " plan right down to platoons the good work is being done. (*See* 43/Training/1278.) But we must stamp out the idea that when a Commander meets with a set-back he piles in more riflemen. He may await darkness or produce smoke, he may bring up more fire power or Tanks (one of them may be the correct answer)—but in the face of modern weapons more men is emphatically the wrong answer.

Ignorance of modern War and lack of resource or imagination must no longer be allowed to masquerade as bulldog determination, or we shall again witness the wasteful methods of the Great War.

LESSON 10.—THE DANGER OF BAD STAFF WORK, AND BAD INTER-COMMUNICATION

The Battle of Gaza should become a classic example of a Battle won by troops, and lost by Staff.

No personal blame attaches to anyone in this respect. Our Army in this theatre could not find adequate Staff and Inter-communication personnel to deal with the situation. The Nation had never made preparation in such respects for a War of this magnitude, or embracing operations in such numerous and varying theatres of War.

The following examples are cited:—

(a) *Bad Staff work.*

    (i) On 26th March, 53rd Division was ordered to withdraw, and to make touch with 54th Division, which was stated to be at Sheikh Abbas; in reality, it had already been moved 4 miles away. This resulted in the giving up of valuable ground, which had to be re-captured next day.

    (ii) The voluntary evacuation of an important position such as Sheikh Abbas is a further instance of bad Staff work.

(b) *Inter-communication.*—Wireless messages saying that the Turks were abandoning Gaza reached Eastern Force Telegraph Exchange at 6.30 p.m., but did not reach the Force Commander until 11 p.m.; had they reached him earlier, the gains made during the day would probably not have been surrendered.

The deduction is that our arrangements for the Peace Training of Staff and Signals were inadequate.

(A) At the beginning of the War the Staff College and other Schools closed down so that all teachers and pupils should go off to see the War and share the glory of a thrilling contest which was only to last a few months. This proved to be unwise.

It is suggested:—

    (i) That there should be arrangements made that Army Schools are capable of expansion the moment mobilization is ordered.

    (ii) That, as it takes longer to train a Staff Officer or Signaller, than other personnel, there should be a proportionally greater reserve of such in Peace Time.

    (iii) That the output of our Staff College should be greater.

(B) Another point is that during the War at periods of stress the Staff were exhausted physically and mentally. This was partly due to unsystematic working of reliefs, partly due to want of trust in Subordinates. It still goes on at Peace Manœuvres. G.S.Os. (I) and Brigade Majors try to sit up all night. This should be stopped.

Lesson 11.—The value of well planned administration

The value of good and well planned administration is of even more importance in semi-civilized tracts than in civilized countries.

The greatest feat in this Campaign up to June, 1917, was the administration conquest of 150 miles of desert. The triumph was over difficulties presented by a harsh unbending nature as much as over Military opposition.

Many clever devices enabled those difficulties to be overcome; for example:—

(a) The spear point pump.
> This went far to solve the horse watering problem.
(b) The ped rail and the use of rabbit wire for overcoming difficulty of getting wheels over soft sand.
(c) The system of water pipe and rail laying evolved.

The Official History of Australia in the War states (Vol. VII, p. 108):—

> "England has fought many desert Campaigns; but Governments enter upon each new war with little or no consideration for lessons of the past." . . . "There was no sanitation at Romani . . . The whole camp was a fly breeding area . . . There were no rakes, spades, shovels, carts, baskets, boxes, bags, or any means of moving manure. No disinfectants, or fly deterrents, or poisons were available."

As the Middle East is a possible theatre of war in the future, it would be of value if all the administrative lessons we learnt in these parts were compiled into one volume. This volume would deal with War Administration in the Middle East. If this is not done Statesmen and Soldiers alike may light-heartedly embark on operations with the lessons of the past forgotten.

Assyrian and Egyptian troops, the soldiers of Alexander, of the Cæsars, and of Napoleon, all traversed this inhospitable land of Sinai. They must all have had their own methods of solving the problems of the desert, yet those methods are as lost to posterity as are the Sybilline Books.

The Manual of Operations on the N.W. Frontier of India is a useful handbook and has the merit of brevity—88 pages. Long manuals are indigestible and not so well mastered as short manuals. A manual of "Operations in the Middle East" would be of value, especially as attention is being paid in training to a major operation in such a theatre.

LESSON 12.—THE DESIRABILITY OF A PLAN OF ATTACK WHICH IS FLEXIBLE, NOT RIGID

At 2nd Gaza our Infantry were stopped by unsubdued machine guns and other small arms. The only resort of the Commander was to put in more riflemen on his front of attack.

The futility of this was seen on other fronts in the Great War.

How can such rigidity of plan be avoided?

The plan should be flexible, *e.g.* : —

(1) The attack may be switched off to another place.

(2) It may be stopped till darkness helps.

(3) A new force of artillery or tanks may be brought in.

The one wrong solution is to pour in more riflemen.

This in previous times may have been evidence of perseverance or determination on the Leader's part. To-day, it is an indication that the Leader does not know his trade.

How are we to train our Leaders to be versatile; to be able to make a plan which will admit of switching off an attack here and on there; to cut losses and run profits; to start a fresh attack instead of pursuing one which has wrecked or got out of control?

The poet wrote of Marlborough that he " taught the doubtful battle how to rage ". Can a leader do this to-day, or has the range of weapons moved the battle too far from the commander? Can we train the young commander to be versatile?

Peace training with its unavoidable absence of the confusion of battle finds the task difficult.

The adoption of a flexible plan, however, may be practised at, say, an assault bridging operation. The wrong way to conduct this operation is to attempt the bridge launching at one place only, and if opposed try to drive through with it in face of opposition regardless of casualties. Such rigidity must not be counted as determination.

The better method is to try two or three separate places— drop the failures like hot cakes—rush the reserve to the place where success is achieved.

This seems only simple sense, but the perpetrator of the wrong method will often get away with his bad rigid plan because he has shown determination and broken no Book principles.

Directors of Exercises might, with advantage, be more watchful as to the Commander's use of reserves, and create sudden changes of situations demanding quick appreciation. It should also be noted if the Commander sticks unduly to his pre-conceived idea or uses his wits.

Battles are won by wits as well as by weapons. Why not develop wits? As the C.I.G.S. put it: " In the last War we were fighting with our fists and bludgeons instead of with our brains and rapiers ".

Too many Exercises are so set as merely to produce a " head-on " collision.

One side defends, one attacks a position. This induces rigidity and is apt to make commanders lose sight of manœuvre, ruse, flexibility of plan, and surprise.

Army Training Memorandum No. 4. A. of 1932 is very welcome. It will induce flexibility of plan.

The commander of a formation, unit or sub-unit must realize early in his career one of the main purposes of keeping a Reserve and of keeping near his Reserve. That purpose is power of manœuvre. He must make no plan so rigid that he forfeits this power. He must be prepared to make a new plan, or change his old plan. He must be prepared to back up whichever of his forward subordinates is making the best head-way. He must rush his reserve there before the enemy has time to plug the breach.

LESSON 14.—IMPORTANCE OF INTER-COMMUNICATION AND TRANS-MISSION OF INFORMATION

1st Battle of Gaza

The difficulty of inter-communication has been emphasized, and the thirst for information which the Higher Commanders feel in order to facilitate control of the battle, and to make fresh plans.

How can we train to improve this?

The answer seems to be " commence at the bottom "; train the young commanders, and see that they know what to do when Commanding the smallest sub-units.

At Field Training a Section or Platoon Leader comes in touch with the enemy. Does he at once think of sending a message to his immediate superior? Does he send the right type of message? Has he thought before-hand how he is going to send it? and the quickest means? and the quickest route? If he has a choice of a H.Q. has he chosen one which facilitate sending of messages? In short, has he a signal sense? Admitting the difficulty of inter-communication in battle, have we done all we can in Peace to inculcate the instinct to communicate? Perhaps we could do more.

At T.E.W.T. the Director can and should see to it that one of the first actions of the pupil on meeting the enemy is " inform my superior ". Only if drummed in almost " ad nauseam " will it become second nature.

The tendency of commanders to be too far back adds to the difficulty of communication. This should not be difficult to eradicate in Peace Training.

One argument in favour of his being back should be suppressed. This is that if forward he interferes with his subordinates. This should not follow, *e.g.*, the commander of the Main Body should be able to be up with his Advanced Guard watching the Advanced Guard battle—without mixing himself in it. In fact, he ought to be watching it hatching the while his own plan. Then if the Advanced Guard attack is held up, the Main Body plan is all the more ready for execution.

At Brigade H.Q. there is a lack of personnel for liaison and inter-communication work.

This is felt especially when working on wide fronts.

Some cyclists should be provided—either 12 per Brigade H.Q. or 3 per Battalion for use at Brigade H.Q.

LESSON 14.—DIFFICULTY OF CONTROL IN BATTLE

1st and 2nd Battles of Gaza

In a modern battle great difficulty is found in retaining control and avoiding breakdown of command once combat is joined and confusion commences.

The war problem which followed this as a corollary was how to convert a " break-in " into a " break-through ".

In peace time we can prepare for the difficulty by encouraging at the right time:—

(1) Decentralization.
(2) Initiative on the part of subordinates.

How can we practise commanders in keeping control once confusion begins?

Some commanders let the battle run itself from the start, before confusion reigns. They are not carrying out their function.

What about the commander who runs it well till confusion sets in? I suggest we should allow tactical operations at training to become confused. Then see what commanders do. Usually we sound the " CEASE FIRE ". I suggest we sound only the " STAND FAST ". This is merely to prevent peace battles going so quick that no chance is given of information finding its way back or of asserting control.

As soon as the Director sees that commanders have got a reasonable amount of information on which to assert control by making a plan he should sound the " CONTINUE ".

I suggest this as a possible device for instructing the commanders of the future to emulate Marlborough and " teach the doubtful battle how to rage ".

LESSON 16.—INCREASED IMPORTANCE OF NIGHT OPERATIONS

Turkish night attacks on the Suez Canal Defences

The main stumbling blocks in the way of the attacker are the defenders machine guns. Though it is obvious that one cannot defeat them by walking up to them, yet attack plans have failed to recognize this elementary truth.

We can deal with these machine guns in three ways:—

(1) Stalking them. This can only be done against weak, or ill organized defence.
(2) Damaging them. Shell, bullet, tank, gas.
(3) Blinding them. Smoke, fog, night.

In spite of their difficulties, attacks by night acquired prominence in the Great War, and it is doubtful whether they are sufficiently practised in peace training.

The main trouble in planning night attacks during the war was probably wire. In peace training the main defect is the want of proper training. Though the technique of night operations is easy, there is a great deal of it, due to the fact that much has to be pre-arranged and ordered, and comparatively little left to the individual judgement.

In most of the training I have seen since the war, much of the technique appears to have been forgotten, and insufficient attention has been paid to such matters.

For example:—

(1) Facility in forming up in the dark.
(2) Slow and regular pace of movement.
(3) Keeping touch with centre.
(4) Keeping distance and interval.
(5) No halting when fired at.
(6) Dealing with flank opposition.

The experiences of the war suggest that with well trained and reliable troops, and with well thought out plans, a night attack is suitable for the stolid unexcitable British soldier.

During peace training night attacks are usually practised in a wrong method. They are made the climax of the operation. This is wrong. They should usually be the prelude to further operations. If his surprise has come off, and his night attack has become a success, the commander has only been successful in a " break-in " to the enemy position. Can he convert this into a " break-through " and a victory? Has he arranged his reserves so as to effect this? I suggest attention be paid to this point when night operations are practised.

It is suggested that when night attacks fail it is usually due to bad pre-arrangement. With good pre-arrangement, and reliable troops, the night attack privides a useful method by which the attack can cut down some of the advantages of the defence.

APPENDIX V

REPORT ON THE MESOPOTAMIAN CAMPAIGN BY MAJOR-GENERAL B. D. FISHER, C.B., C.M.G., D.S.O., AND MAJOR-GENERAL C. C. ARMITAGE, C.M.G., D.S.O.

ARRANGEMENT OF REPORT

NOTE

This report does not contain any lessons which, in the writers' opinion, have been thoroughly and accurately incorporated in our training manuals of today. It should be remembered that deductions from the Mesopotamian Campaign are affected by the Turks' relative want of machine guns, and their comparative incapacity in handling them.

PART I.—PEACE PREPARATION

1. *The cost paid by a nation which goes to war unprepared*

The numerous mistakes made by the British Empire in all theatres were chiefly attributable to the fact that it was not prepared for war.

In peace-time all possible operations should be studied and plans made for all eventualities. The perfect co-operation of the Navy, Army and Air Force in these plans should be assured.

Had proper steps been taken in peace to study the possibilities of a war in Mesopotamia, a large number of mistakes and much loss of life would have been avoided.

In the same way as preparations for, and study in peace of, all campaigns are carried out under the orders of the C.I.G.S. so must the supreme control of conduct of all operations remain under the War Office. For the first eighteen months of this campaign the War Office did not exercise such control. The campaign was thus allowed to develop into an isolated military enterprise.

2. *The equipment of the army with the most modern means of waging war*

It is of the greatest importance that our army should be equipped with the most modern armaments for its next war.

Only by superior morale, equipment, training and organization can a civilized power deal successfully with a second-class enemy.

If the use of heavy guns and tanks is denied to us, as appears to be possible, we shall be seriously handicapped, for at the present time practically all semi-civilized people are equipped with modern rifles and machine guns, and it is not possible to deal with these unless on our part every modern means of waging war is brought into effect.

PART II.—STRATEGICAL AND TACTICAL LESSONS

1. *The inter-dependence of policy and strategy*

The necessity of keeping policy and strategy in harmony was brought out very clearly in the campaign in Mesopotamia, and at a heavy cost. Policy and strategy were subject to dual control from England and India, with the result that policy in Mesopotamia, viewed purely in a local light, assumed an undue importance and demanded the advance to Bagdad, which strategically was unsound. Consequently our forces strove to gain an end that politically was a luxury and strategically was of little value, and which hampered our efforts in the main theatre of war.

Policy and strategy should be inter-dependent and if one authority cannot control both, the authority which dictates the policy must have an intimate knowledge of strategy, or must give full weight to strategical considerations as put forward by the proper adviser.

These points are dealt with very briefly in F.S.R. II, Chap. I, Sec. 3, para. 4, and a clear statement of the principles involved should be available for the Committee of Imperial Defence in the form of a special paper or pamphlet, if this has not already been done.

2. *The inter-dependence of strategy, tactics and administration*

The campaign in Mesopotamia proved clearly that unless strategy, tactics and administration are inter-dependent, disaster will ensue.

In the first two years of the campaign policy had become too ambitious; to carry out the policy it was necessary for our forces to advance up the river Tigris. The necessary transportation services and administrative organization did not exist. Supplies and medical stores were deficient, and transport to carry them was inadequate; added to which the climate was bad, and at times of the year parts of the country became inundated.

Nevertheless policy asked, and strategy and tactics permitted the advance to continue, in spite of the ever lengthening communications. So long as the enemy put up no determined resistance the advance could continue, though the supply system became worse, and the method of evacuating the sick left much to be desired.

Eventually the enemy, having been reinforced, turned and fought with determination; although Townshend gained a tactical success at Ctesiphon on 22nd November, 1915, it resulted in a strategical defeat of the first magnitude, and the despatch of relieving forces became necessary. The administrative system broke down completely; troops were not sure of supplies; casualties were evacuated after long delays under terrible conditions, and their large number further congested the transport system; the result was that an administrative disaster took place, which has hardly ever been equalled in the history of the British Army.

The reason of this was that a strategical plan had been evolved without due consideration of its administrative feasibility; neither had climate, topographic, nor hygienic factors been considered.

This campaign shows only too clearly the risk of embarking on any strategical or tactical operation without an assured system of supply; the more prolonged the operation and the longer the line of communication the surer must be the system.

The above is purely a military question, and should be more fully dealt with in F.S.R. I and II.

3. *Tactical surprise*

The greatest lesson to be gathered from the campaign is that no attack in modern war is feasible—or likely to succeed—against an enemy in position, unless his resisting power has already been paralysed either : —

    (*a*) by some form of surprise, or
    (*b*) by preponderating fire, powerful enough to produce the effect of surprise.

In the campaign in Mesopotamia, owing to all troops being more or less tied to their water supply, the power of the defence was somewhat weakened by the fact that there was generally an " open flank ". Most of the successful engagements were planned on the turning of this flank, *e.g.*, Ramadi, Tikrit, etc.

Our training manuals require to emphasize far more strongly the vital importance of surprise and of the indirect approach, and the danger of a direct or frontal attack against a defensive position—however hastily organized—when the element of

surprise is absent. Surprise may be obtained in various ways—
by deceiving the enemy as to the time and place of attack, by
the use of new weapons such as gas or tanks, by taking
advantage of opportunities offered by darkness, fog and rain,
or by adopting any unexpected method of making war.
F.S.R. II, might well contain a sentence to the effect that a
commander who embarks on an offensive against a prepared
position and fails to surprise his opponent, has lost the main
advantage which the offensive confers.

Too much stress cannot be given to the subject of surprise
in all forms of training in peace. At present our methods are
inclined to be too stereotyped, and originality during field training is often discouraged by higher commanders.

4. *The power of the machine gun and automatic weapon in Defence*

The chief tactical lesson of the campaign is the dominating
power of the machine gun and automatic weapon in defence.

The problem of the attack is that of the unlocated hostile
machine gun. In the Great War this problem was eventually
overcome by the use of a mass of artillery and of tanks. Such
a mass of artillery is not available today, and the antidote to the
tank is slowly evolving. On the other hand machine guns have
increased since the war both in numbers and technical efficiency.

How then is infantry to regain its power in the attack? The
answer seems to be in the development by the infantry of the
highest possible state of training, so that full use can be made of
the offensive power of the rifle, and when possible the machine
gun, supplemented by adequate support of mortars, artillery
and tanks.

With the present cumbersome Lewis gun and Vickers
machine gun little progress can be made. The advent of a dual
purpose gun, which will combine the light and heavy machine
gun in one weapon with separate mountings offers a possible
solution to the problem.

The rifle company should be organized afresh, so as to give
full scope to the offensive power of the rifle and light machine
gun. The rifleman should be lightly equipped, and fully mobile.
Full use should be made of mechanization to give mobility,
invulnerability, and ample ammunition supply to all machine
guns, but the smallest possible number of vehicles should be
used, and the machines should be simple armoured carriers
only.

The battalion should be supported by stokes mortars firing
H.E., smoke, and gas, the function of which should be to deal
with the unexpected hostile machine gun, which is immune to
artillery fire. The exact organization of these mortars can only
be settled after experiment, but they must be mechanized.

The intimate co-operation of artillery and tanks with infantry must be assured as in the past, and these arms must be sufficiently powerful and numerous to carry out their task efficiently.

5. *Infantry attacks over open ground*

The operations for the relief of Kut involved a series of frontal attacks against an entrenched enemy in daylight, and over open ground which offered neither covered approaches nor facilities for manœuvre in the attack.

At first infantry attempted to provide their own covering fire by advancing in a series of rushes in accordance with pre-war training. The result was that these attacks were slowed up at ranges of 1,000 yards or more, and were eventually brought to a standstill 800 yards or more from their objectives. The solution in the end was found to be a non-stop attack by the infantry, covering fire being found by other means.

Should similar conditions occur again, it must be accepted that the rôle of infantry committed to the capture of objectives is to continue to advance, and that their power to do so is dependent entirely on the support afforded them by other arms or other bodies of troops.

6. *The " break-in " and the " break-through "*

By this is meant the importance and the difficulty of prompt exploitation, and the momentum of the maintenance of the attack long enough to prevent the enemy rallying, or cementing the breach. Many instances occurred in Mesopotamia, where hostile positions could be broken *into*, but could not be broken *through*, before the enemy's reserves were able to arrive and repair the breach. The inability to " break-through " was caused by this inability to follow up quickly enough, and was due to the lack of an arm possessing sufficient tactical mobility. In the past cavalry had been this arm, but fire power—chiefly in the shape of machine guns—has very largely destroyed their mobility on the battlefield, with the result that battles have become indecisive. Hence there is a definite need to recreate a tactically mobile formation—possibly of all arms—under a selected commander with proper staff and signals; against a reputable foe it is held that a large proportion of such a formation must be armoured or partially armoured.

It is suggested that—as an aid to exploitation—our training manuals and exercises should devote more attention to the action and leading of reserve units.

F.S.R. II, Sec. 75, deals with the " break-through " under the heading of " The Final Phases ", and dismisses the subject

G 2

in three paragraphs. The whole of this section requires rewriting, and some attempt made to reproduce in cold print the confusion and fog of war, which are inevitable at this phase of the battle, and to portray the possibilities for initiative, bold leadership and command.

7. *The value of ground*

The possession of commanding ground has always been of great value in military operations, and the lessons of the Great War only serve to confirm this fact. In Mesopotamia the ground enormously favoured the defence; the lack of all landmarks, the mirage, and the ease with which digging could be carried out all assisted the defence. The advantages of surprise are on the side of the army which holds commanding ground, without it artillery is deprived of a large part of its power, and the advent of survey methods and of air observation has only affected the problem in a minor degree.

The moral effect on infantry and indeed on all troops, when placed in defensive positions on ground commanded by the enemy, is very harmful.

But while appreciating these obvious facts our training manuals must not over-emphasize them, otherwise the result will be that in attack efforts will always be made to capture the highest ground, while in defence artillery observation posts will invariably be sited on hills with the infantry in the low ground beneath. The experiences of Mesopotamia show that a very powerful defence can be made without the possession of commanding ground.

In the attack commanding positions can generally be turned, while in defence it is more advantageous to hold gently undulating ground, the valleys of which face the enemy, thus depriving his artillery of positions, than to occupy hills which give an obvious target to the hostile artillery. Concealment of infantry positions is essential.

In the " gaining of contact " phase, F.S.R. II, Sec. 62. 4, states—" Such positions are likely to be the most strongly defended, and it is against them that the attacker must develop his maximum fire power ". This paragraph requires revision, as the principle of attempting to gain prominent and strongly defended features is under modern conditions generally a fallacy.

Finally we must rid ourselves of the obsession all too prevalent in many theatres of the Great War, that ground is of itself of any value. Many instances occurred of the high command's rather unintelligible reluctance to relinquish any ground, which had once been occupied—irrespective of whether it was really vital to our operations. Many thousands of lives were thus lost for the sake of holding or re-capturing by counter-attack ground of only sentimental value. If the enemy has a great advantage of ground, a withdrawal should be carried out to a position, where the conditions are not so disadvantageous. A well planned withdrawal does not lower the morale of troops, but on the contrary inspires them with confidence in their commanders, and offers opportunities for a counter-offensive.

8. *The counter-attack*

In spite of the very clear lessons of the war a great deal of confusion of thought still exists in regard to the counter-attack. Our manuals do not emphasise sufficiently clearly the great difference between the immediate, and the deliberate counter-attack.

The immediate counter-attack is nothing more than a platoon and company affair, its object being to stabilize the situation on the defensive front with the aid of the supporting fire immediately available. Provided that the enemy advance is stopped and the situation is again stabilized, it is not of vital importance that the original position held by the defence should be re-captured. The Turks used this form of counter-attack with effect on occasions (c/f the expedition and skill with which their counter-attacks were delivered during the clearing of the Khadairi Bend).

The re-establishment of a new defensive front is effected by means of the deliberate counter-attack, which is a matter for reserve formations— all arms being concerned. Its object is to restore the situation by offensive action after due preparation by the use of all available supporting arms.

The difference between the immediate and the deliberate counter-attack is thus a matter of—

(*a*) time of delivery,
(*b*) object, and
(*c*) troops employed.

These points are not clear in F.S.R. Vol. II, Sec. 82, and Infantry Training Vol. II, Sec. 26. The wording of F.S.R. II, Sec. 62 (2) lines 9 to 13 is, in fact, somewhat confusing.

9. *Information and communications*

Throughout the war many instances occurred of the higher command being completely out of touch with subordinate commanders, and their failing to issue orders for the pressing home of the attack (of the total failure of communication between Divisional H.Q. at Nukhailat and Column " A " at the Battle of Kut, 28th September, 1915). In any case it must be realized that however accurate, early, and frequent may be the reports received from those engaged in the actual fighting, it is essential that they should be reinforced by a system of " Liaison Forward " as the only way to obtain information in time for the issue of orders for exploitation, launching of counter-attacks and other matters. All superior commanders should therefore have liaison personnel, whose sole task is to report on the situation, as it affects both the enemy and our own troops.

These reports will not in any way absolve commanders of lower formations from reporting on the situation in the usual way. But such reports are only of use if communications are reliable. When communications fail, command fails. The improvement and simplification of existing means of communication are therefore essential.

The advent of wireless and the motor-cycle has up to now resulted in no appreciable saving in the use of the telephone and cable. The presence of track machines has rendered communication by cable in the forward areas most precarious.

If all ranks are given a more thorough training in " Signal sense ", and if the use of—

(i) liaison personnel emanating forward from every formation,

(ii) motor-cycle D.Rs., and

(iii) wireless are developed, there will be less difficulty in maintaining communication in the forward areas.

The use of cable in these areas may be possible in peace, but it is impracticable in war.

It is recommended that cable should be abolished in front of infantry brigade H.Q. except in the case of artillery units. The result of this will be a more certain maintenance of communications in all conditions and a far more efficient system in mobile warfare.

10. *Counter-offensive*

Our training manuals do not sufficiently emphasize the possibilities and value of a counter-offensive, followed a withdrawing manœuvre. The action of a force deliberately withdrawing, with a view to laying a trap or drawing the enemy into a trap, must often possess the chance of obtaining a decisive success. The conduct and organization of such an operation require practice and attention in our peace training, *e.g.*, the chance which lay with Nur-ud-Kin at the time of the battle of Ctesiphon, where with the arrival of Turkish reinforcements, he could have drawn General Townshend even further towards Baghdad and then turned and annihilated him.

11. *Night operations*

The campaign in Mesopotamia clearly proved the value of operations at night in a country where landmarks were practically non-existent. Both at Dujaila and at the first Sannaiyat, the part of the operations which took place in the dark was successful. In both cases it was daylight that produced disaster. The advance of the III Corps to the Hai, and the approach to the Khaidari Bend were night operations of great success.

The great importance of a cloak of obscurity, either darkness, fog, or artificial smoke, should be stressed, and in our training more attention should be paid to: —

(*a*) moving at night on wide frontages;
(*b*) working in foggy weather, and
(*c*) the use of the compass. In this connection an urgent need exists for the invention of a new design of compass, which is not affected by or dependent on the vagaries of geological conditions.

In the peace training to-day night operations are apt to be of too stereotyped and routine a nature, and are often only carried out with the primary object of bringing them to a conclusion at the earliest possible opportunity. A general change of mentality is required as regards the importance of night operations, and all ranks must be made to realize how much the keeping down of casualties and the whole success of operations will depend in future on the high standard of training and efficiency attained in this respect in peace time.

12. *The maintenance of morale*

The morale of the troops in Mesopotamia was lowered during the early part of the campaign by poor food, inadequate medical arrangements, lack of leave, bad postal services and the effect—especially on the Indian troops—of the loneliness and isolation of the desert. The troops thus affected were well trained and disciplined units.

The maintenance of morale is one of the primary functions of commanders and of the staff, particularly of the administrative staff. Defective administration and lack of forethought on the part of the administrative staff may have as great an effect in lowering morale as defeat in battle. This matter should be dealt with more thoroughly in F.S.R. I and II.

13. *Cavalry*

The outstanding failure of the cavalry, at the commencement of the Mesopotamian Campaign was due not only to poor leadership, faulty instruction and weakness of their fire power, but to neglect of not making full use of their mobility, *e.g.,* the action of the cavalry brigade at the Battle of Dujaila and that of the cavalry division at the Shumran Bend. It must be remembered that except for dependence on the river for water, the country favoured wide movements, and every advantage lay with the mounted arm. The contrast, afforded by the success of the cavalry in the last year of the Mesopotamian Campaign, *e.g.*, Ramadi, is worthy of note. It was the same cavalry, the same material, there was no great difference in the ground.

The main lesson to be learnt is that when dealing with a highly mobile force, the question of the selection, energy and physical fitness of the commander, and the issue of the correct instructions assume an even greater importance than under normal conditions.

PART III.—ORGANIZATION AND EQUIPMENT

1. *The lightening of the load of the infantry soldier*

The enormous load carried by the Infantry soldier in the Great War, deprived him of his fighting ability and made him into a beast of burden only able to close with the enemy, when put there by the fire of the other arms.

The first essential is to give back to the infantryman his mobility, and permit him once again to be able to fight forward with his own weapons, without being entirely dependent on the support of other arms.

The advent of mechanization will enable this to be done with reasonable chances of success.

2. *The covering fire problem*

Although everything possible should be done to train and organize infantry units, so that they can fight their way forward in suitable country with their own weapons, it is obvious that— with the power of the machine gun in defence—it is necessary to have adequate fire power available to enable infantry to attack under any conditions, when the situation demands it. This additional fire power is given by artillery and tanks, the former being the more general form of support.

With only three Field Brigades R.A. in the divisional artillery it is not possible to put down fire on more than about 1,000 yards of front, and at the same time adequately to deal with the flanks. It is most desirable that an extra field brigade R.A. should be added to the divisional artillery, but this is a difficult matter in these days of reduction and economy.

The advent of the mortar as an infantry weapon offers a solution to the question. The mortar will take over the greater part of the functions of the 3·7 howitzer, and it should now be possible to consider the conversion of light brigades R.A. into field artillery, in order to give the necessary increase to the field artillery of the division.

In connection with the covering fire problem it is for consideration whether the proportion of howitzers should not be increased. The present proportion of howitzers to guns in field brigades is a low one, and high angle fire is very desirable. By turning light brigades R.A. into field brigades equipped entirely with field howitzers, the proportion of high angle fire will be increased. The brigades can always be re-equipped with 3·7 howitzers, if required for service on the Indian Frontier, or in any other part of the world suitable to them.

Finally the present complicated situation in regard to artillery ammunition should be clarified. Mechanized transport has given to us the solution of the problem of supplying the ever increasing quantities of ammunition required in modern war, but with the continued use of shrapnel by field artillery the number of types of ammunition in the field is excessive, and the complications ensuing in war are a source of danger. Only by the total abolition of shrapnel for field artillery can simplicity be attained, and no serious tactical objection can be raised to this step. Any technical objections that may be raised can be overcome. This change will make for simiplicity in the training both of the infantry and of the artillery.

The position regarding tanks must also be reviewed. The present proportion of tanks to other arms is a low one and does not meet accepted standards of modern war.

PART IV.—ADMINISTRATION

1. *The special study of Eastern theatres of war from the administrative point of view*

A special study of all possible Eastern theatres of war should be made in peace from the point of view of administration.

The information so obtained should be collected in suitable form, and be available on the outbreak of war. Our experiences in the Great War in all parts of the World were bought at a heavy price, and must not be lost.

2. *The importance of the transportation services*

The campaign demonstrated in a remarkable way the complete dependence of operations on adequate means of transportation. This is a truism, but the fact that Commanders and Staff Officers require to possess a sound working knowledge of the limitations and requirements of the transportation services is still perhaps not always fully appreciated.

The officers responsible for the organization and operation of these services are usually drawn from civil life, and it is suggested that more consideration might be given, at Administrative Exercises, to the nature of the instructions they require to receive, in order to enable them to meet the requirements of the Army.

PART V.—TRAINING

1. *The training of the commander and staffs*

On many of the battle fronts of the World War the physical fitness of our commanders and staffs was at fault, *e.g.,* General Nixon's own statement to the Mesopotamian Commission as to why he did not take executive command of the operations at Ctesiphon, p. 72, Vol. II, Mesopotamian Campaign. Is sufficient attention being paid in our training today to this very important subject, remembering that in war physical and mental qualifications are of equal importance? From Mesopotamia, as from every other theatre of war, the necessity of an adequate supply of trained staff officers stands out as one of the most important lessons.

2. *The training of the infantry arm*

The climate, the undeveloped state of the country, and the nature of the earlier operations in Mesopotamia combined to intensify the strain to which the troops were subjected. Whilst this applied to all arms, it must be admitted that the strain on the infantry was more prolonged and heavier than on any other arm.

In view of the importance of the infantry arm it is essential that its morale and training should be maintained at the highest pitch possible. Unfortunately since the war several factors have arisen that have tended to give the infantryman a form of inferiority, when comparing himself with other arms. Chief among those factors are:—

    (i) *Tanks.*—Up to the present infantry have felt more or less powerless against tanks; this, however, is only a passing phase, and the fact should be impressed on infantry that in war weapons will be available, which will enable them to oppose the tank successfully.

    (ii) *Establishments.*—Battalions at home are kept considerably under establishment, as compared with other arms. This has a lowering effect on morale.

    (iii) *Routine duties.*—Most of the extra-regimental employments are found by the infantry and, while still further reducing their numbers for training, this fact is apt to give them the impression that their rôle is a menial one.

It is essential to combat these factors at all times in peace training, and to keep uppermost in the mind of the infantryman that without him wars cannot be won; that in fact he is the man we rely upon to win the next war.

It is no good impressing on infantry that they can do things in war, which at present are quite impossible. It is chiefly the question of the attack against a first class enemy. The infantryman sees the following developments since the war:—

(i) The multiplication of M.Gs. and increase in their efficiency (*i.e.*, an increase in the power of the defence).

(ii) The very considerable reduction in our artillery (*i.e.*, a decrease in the power of attack).

(iii) The rapid progress in power and performance of tanks (*i.e.*, a serious threat to infantry both in attack and defence).

There is no lack of verbal encouragement and exhortation to the infantryman to fight his way forward with his own weapons. The infantryman who actually spent the war in units is naturally sceptical. If infantry are to regain their self-confidence, they must be given concrete proofs in peace that what is expected of them is possible.

Infantry want:—

(i) *Armament and equipment* with which they can fight as infantrymen. A light equipment, loose clothing, light M.Gs., mechanized transport to carry all surplus equipment and ammunition, and some form of close support weapon to deal with enemy M.Gs. Infantry will never be convinced that M.Gs. alone can give them really efficient supporting fire in the attack.

(ii) *Supporting fire.*—Sufficient supporting fire from artillery and tanks to enable them to capture on a limited frontage any position however strongly held, when the situation demands such measures.

(iii) *Trained rifle companies and full establishments.*—It is true to say that rifle companies do very little training at home owing to lack of men; yet the training of the rifle company is most important, and at present it is the least trained sub-unit within the battalion. This is due to a variety of causes which are well known. The rifle company of the future should be highly trained and very mobile unit, capable of developing its full fire power rapidly and effectively. The personnel of rifle companies should be skilled in the use of ground, and should be able to exploit to the fullest extent possible the advantages of darkness, fog, smoke and gas. They should have a thorough knowledge of the support to be expected from artillery and tanks, and know when such support can be dispensed with. They must be taught to realize that supporting arms will not completely destroy the enemy, but will paralyse him for a short period during which the attacker will not be under aimed fire. This is the infantry-man's chance, and he must seize it quickly. Far more time should be made available than has been done in the past to give the individual rifleman a knowledge of warcraft and scout-craft. The whole of the difficulties that now exist at home are due to lack of men. It is essential that battalions should be kept up to establishment. The present constant shortage of man-power is responsible for the lack of training in battalions.

(iv) *Suitable ground.*—It is obviously absurd to tell infantry to attack a well armed enemy over open country in daylight. They can only do so with overwhelming artillery or tank support. This will rarely be available in war; therefore the infantry must very rarely be asked to do it in peace. Suitable enclosed country should, when possible, be provided for training, or, when this is not possible, far more training should be carried out at night, dusk, dawn, or in foggy weather. The daylight attack with inadequate supporting fire against M.Gs. in position is anathema.

(v) *An efficient anti-tank weapon.*—Enough has been seen of the green and white flag. The average infantry-man is beginning to believe that it is not possible to make an anti-tank gun that is efficient. He does not particularly want it himself, but he must be convinced that it exists.

There are also other difficulties with which the infantry are faced:—

(i) *Routine duties and extra-regimental employ.*—This is still the almost exclusive burden of the infantry and is most discouraging; at the same time it further reduces numbers. It should be realized that infantry to-day is the most complex arm, the most difficult to train, requires the longest period of training, and as high a level of education and intelligence as any other arm.

The only just and satisfactory solution is to place all arms of the service (including signals and R.E.) on exactly the same footing, and to regulate demands for working parties and extra-regimental employ by the strengths of units and the relation of strength to establishment, and by no other criterion.

(ii) *Lack of a policy for the mechanization of infantry.*— After the experience and experiments of the past few years the time is approaching when it should be possible to frame a definite policy for the mechanization of infantry battalions. The advent of mechanization must not be allowed still further to complicate the battalion organization. The number of machines in a battalion must be kept down to a minimum and the simplest possible form of mechanized organization must be introduced, easily adaptable to and economical in any part of the Empire.

3. *The fog of war*

In all mobile operations the fog of war is always present. But in peace training, when the forces on both sides are known, the element of surprise is often absent. Far more can be done to introduce this fog of war in the training of commanders and troops in peace. A little foresight and imagination on the part of directors of exercises will bring the unexpected into the picture, and give more reality to training. Training in night operations should be general, as this gives a far truer picture of war than operations by day.

4. *Orders and instructions*

The more rigid the type of warfare, the more formal and precise can orders be. In mobile operations, however, precise orders cannot be issued to meet every possibility, and commanders will have to act on general instructions. All commanders should, therefore, be trained to work at times on instructions, and not to rigid orders.

The whole tendency of our manuals and teaching since the war has been to lay too much stress on the importance of orders as such. F.S.R. II, Chap. XII, glorifies the precise and formal written order. Operation instructions are only treated as personal and exceptional things, and the necessity for the frequent issue of brief verbal orders or instructions is hardly dealt with.

The result of this teaching is that many officers are apt to be misled into thinking that, once a written order has been issued, everything will work out satisfactorily. Nothing could be more dangerous or further from the truth. F.S.R. II, Chap. XII, should be re-written on broader lines, and sanction should be given to the more general issue of instructions instead of orders, and to the use of verbal orders confirmed in writing when time permits. It is very desirable that staff officers should be taught to write perfect orders. It is most undesirable that commanders should have their hands tied by formalism in this matter.

(B40/180)   125   4/40   W.O.P.   5101